James K. Boyce

Investing in Peace: Aid and Conditionality after Civil Wars

Adelphi Paper 351

Oxford University Press, Great Clarendon Street, Oxford OX2 6DP
Oxford   New York
Athens   Auckland   Bangkok   Bombay   Calcutta   Cape Town
Dar es Salaam   Delhi   Florence   Hong Kong   Istanbul   Karachi
Kuala Lumpur   Madras   Madrid   Melbourne   Mexico City
Nairobi   Paris   Taipei   Tokyo   Toronto
and associated companies in
Berlin   Ibadan

Oxford is a trade mark of Oxford University Press

Published in the United States
by Oxford University Press Inc., New York

First published September 2002 by **Oxford University Press for
The International Institute for Strategic Studies**
Arundel House, 13–15 Arundel Street, Temple Place, London WC2R 3DX
www.iiss.org

Director John Chipman
Editor Mats R. Berdal
Assistant Editor Glen Quatermain

British Library Cataloguing in Publication Data
Data available

Library of Congress Cataloguing in Publication Data

ISBN 0-19-851669-x
ISSN 0567-932x

Contents

Glossary

AHLC	Ad Hoc Liaison Committee
AIPAC	American Israel Public Affairs Committee
CPP	Cambodian People's Party
CG	Consultative Group
EBRD	European Bank for Reconstruction and Development
ETF	Economic Task Force
EU	European Union
EUAM	European Union Administration for Mostar
Funcinpec	United National Front for an Independent, Neutral, Peaceful, and Cooperative Cambodia
GDP	gross domestic product
KR	Khmer Rouge
ICG	International Crisis Group
IDB	Inter-American Development Bank
IFIs	international financial institutions
IFOR	Implementation Force
IMF	International Monetary Fund
MINUGUA	United Nations Verification Mission in Guatemala
NGO	non-governmental organisation
OECD	Organisation for Economic Cooperation and Development
OHR	Office of the High Representative
PA	Palestinian Authority
PLO	Palestine Liberation Organisation

RENAMO	Mozambique National Resistance
RRTF	Reconstruction and Return Task Force
SFOR	Stabilisation Force
SNC	Supreme National Council
UNDP	United Nations Development Programme
UNHCR	UN High Commissioner for Refugees
UNITA	National Union for the Total Independence of Angola
UNTAC	United Nations Transitional Authority in Cambodia
URNG	Guatemalan National Revolutionary Unity
USAID	US Agency for International Development
VAT	value-added tax

Introduction

Civil wars often end in a negotiated peace accord rather than outright victory for either side. Yet the 'peace' of these accords usually is more a statement of intent, or hope, than an accomplished fact. The contests for power that animated war do not disappear with a peace accord, and the risks of renewed violence can persist long after the agreement is signed. Rather than a definitive end to war, an accord should be seen as a tentative step towards peace. It marks the beginning of a new stage in the war-to-peace transition typically referred to as 'peace-building'. The peace accord is at best a rough blueprint, with the final outcome uncertain. Whether a lasting peace will be constructed depends crucially on what happens next.

In the 1990s, peace-building became a major growth industry for aid agencies, non-governmental organisations (NGOs), and many governments. With the ink scarcely dry on the peace accords, donors pledged large sums for 'peace implementation', or the carrying out of formally agreed peace accords, and for 'post-war reconstruction', or the rebuilding of infrastructure in war-torn territories. In Cambodia, for example, the 1991 Paris Peace Agreement unlocked more than $3 billion (bn) in external assistance. The 1993 Oslo Accord was followed by more than $4bn in aid pledges for the Palestinians. One week after the signing of the Dayton Peace Agreement in 1995, the World Bank and European Union (EU) unveiled a $5bn reconstruction programme for Bosnia at a donor conference in Brussels. All told, multilateral and bilateral aid agencies pledged more than $100bn in so-called 'post-conflict' assistance to some three dozen war-torn countries in the past decade. Looking ahead, the UN's initial cost estimate for 'rebuilding Afghanistan' is at least $6.5bn over the next five years.[1]

Yet the impact of external assistance on war-torn societies is uncertain. Aid does not necessarily act like water on the embers of conflict, effectively helping to extinguish further hostilities. It can add fuel to the fire. Six years after the Dayton agreement, Bosnia's nationalist parties continue to dominate the country's political life, having propped themselves up in part by diverting funds from public utilities that received substantial foreign aid. The country's power plants and transportation infrastructure have been repaired, but Bosnia remains effectively partitioned into three ethnically 'cleansed' mini-states. One result is that despite the billions of dollars in aid, international troops are still essential to prevent a return to war.

Back in the donor countries, domestic support for such aid is showing signs of waning when faced with its mounting costs and its often disappointing results. Foreign aid has never been the most popular of causes among taxpayers, and after spending billions of dollars on aid to war-torn societies, with no apparent end in sight, public disillusionment and 'donor fatigue' threaten to undercut future aid efforts.

Peace conditionality

This paper explores one avenue that has been proposed to make external assistance a more effective instrument for establishing a viable peace: 'peace conditionality.' The term 'peace conditionality' was coined in a 1995 study of economic policy in El Salvador, which recommended that the World Bank and the International Monetary Fund (IMF) make their aid conditional on steps taken by the Salvadoran government to mobilise its own resources to fund high-priority peace programmes.[2] Like other types of conditionality, peace conditionality involves using aid as a 'carrot' to encourage specific steps by the recipients. But whereas the central aims of 'conventional' conditionality – most commonly associated with the Bretton Woods institutions – have focused principally on achieving short-term macroeconomic stability and long-term economic reform, the central aims of peace conditionality are the short-term implementation of peace accords and the long-term consolidation of peace.

In one sense, the pledges of aid after a peace accord are conditional from their very inception: the signing of the accord itself is a precondition for the aid. The subsequent disbursement of aid is also inherently conditional, insofar as a resumption of conflict would trigger its suspension and failure to make tangible progress toward peace would jeopardise new aid commitments. The aim of peace conditionality is to move beyond these limited choices, in which the aid tap is either 'on' or 'off', and to link the flow of aid more closely to movement towards a lasting peace. Peace conditionality can be implemented by means of formal performance criteria, such as explicit targets for cuts in military expenditure specified in the texts of aid agreements, or by means of informal policy dialogue between aid donors and recipients, in which the links between aid and specific measures by the recipients are not spelt out on paper. In either case, the aim is to get more 'non-bang for the buck'.[3] Achieving a lasting peace is seldom easy, and donors must retain sufficient flexibility to adapt both the flow of aid and the conditions that accompany that aid to changing circumstances, rather than sticking to mechanical formulae.

Conditional aid to war-torn societies can address a variety of issues related to the implementation of peace accords and the consolidation of peace. Some of these issues mesh more readily with the usual concerns of aid agencies than do others. For example, the international financial institutions (IFIs) are accustomed to providing advice on fiscal matters, and they are not averse to attaching conditions to the assistance that they provide in order to ensure that their advice is followed. The recommendation that they should apply their leverage to reorient government spending from the military to peace implementation remains controversial, however. Peace-building is a 'political' issue, and many IFI officials maintain that such matters fall outside their mandate to address 'economic' concerns. Yet in practice, no hard-and-fast line separates the two. Economic decisions often have political repercussions and vice versa. If the peace accords unravel and war resumes, hopes for economic recovery are likely to be dashed; and if economic policies fail to bring about broad-based improvements in living standards, the peace process is likely to be imperiled. Recognition of this interdependence led the IFIs to use conditionality to encourage the Guatemalan government to carry out fiscal reforms to implement the 1996 peace accord.

On some occasions, peace conditionality has been applied to issues that further stretch aid agencies' usual interpretations of their mandates. In 1997, for example, the US Congress passed legislation at the urging of human rights groups that directed the Clinton administration to oppose IFI loans to any country or entity that refused to cooperate with the International Criminal Tribunal for the Former Yugoslavia. After the US government moved on this basis to block hundreds of millions of dollars in IMF and World Bank loans to Croatia, the Tudjman government handed over ten individuals who had been indicted for crimes during the war in Bosnia to stand trial in The Hague. This example suggests that where there is the will to exercise peace conditionality, even for objectives that go beyond the scope of past practice, a way can be found.

Ironically, even as some in the aid agencies, NGOs, and donor governments are exploring the potential to reorient conditionality to prevent a resumption of hostilities, others are advocating an across-the-board retreat from conditionality. In response to studies that cast doubt on the effectiveness of the conventional macroeconomic conditionality employed by the IFIs, which suggest that successful reforms cannot be imposed from outside, some are calling for the abandonment of conditionality in favour of 'selectivity'. Rather than pressing unwelcome conditions on reluctant borrowers, it is argued that donors could make better use of scarce resources by targeting aid to countries that have already adopted 'good' economic policies. The demonstration effect of the good performers might then induce countries with 'poor' policies to follow suit.[4] Whatever the merits of selectivity over macroeconomic conditionality, this prescription offers little guidance to appropriate policies during war-to-peace transitions. In the aftermath of a civil war, there typically is little consensual 'ownership' of domestic policies. Some groups are likely to favour one set of policies, other groups another – in a context where disagreements have recently led to large-scale bloodshed. Even peace accords that enjoy a high degree of across-the-board domestic support can prove contentious in their implementation.

Investing in peace is not simply a matter of infrastructure rehabilitation, economic development, or macroeconomic stability, all of which count among the more familiar objectives of the various aid agencies. Nor can peace be pursued most effectively merely as a by-product of these conventional goals. In war-torn societies, donors must move beyond business as usual and take peace-building as a distinct objective that poses distinctive challenges.

The argument in brief

The core argument of this paper is that peace conditionality can be a useful policy tool after negotiated endings to civil wars. Two caveats are necessary, however. First, to argue that peace should figure prominently among donor objectives is not to say that it should invariably override all other objectives when trade-offs arise. In some cases it may not be possible to secure peace at any reasonable cost. In others, conflict can help to launch a society on to a more economically inclusive and politically sustainable path; the struggle against apartheid in South Africa is a case in point. In many cases, however, investment in peace can yield impressive returns, not only in economic terms but also in terms of the broader dimensions of human well-being.

Second, peace conditionality is not a 'magic bullet'. Even when conditionality is necessary to secure a lasting peace, it may not be sufficient. The conflict may be too intractable, the peace accords may not offer a viable blueprint for building a lasting peace, or external support for peace may be inadequate. Moreover, conditionality of any stripe is subject to the political prejudices of donor governments. Yet to acknowledge that peace conditionality is not a panacea is not to say that it is worthless.

The remainder of this paper is organised as follows. The first chapter discusses the strengths and weaknesses of conditionality as an instrument for building peace, drawing in particular on post-Dayton experiences in Bosnia where possibilities for peace conditionality have sparked much debate and some experimentation.

The analysis suggests that while the aid 'carrot' can be sliced so as to strengthen incentives for peace implementation, this is not a straightforward task. Aid-for-peace bargains must not only be accepted by the recipients, but also enforced by the donors. So far, we have only witnessed the first halting steps in what may prove to be a lengthy process of trial and error.

Chapter 2 delves further into a central issue confronting aid agencies in war-torn societies: how to ensure that aid reduces tensions rather than exacerbating them. In the short term, donors must try to sustain the balances of power among the parties to the conflict, so that no side is tempted to return to war, either to seek an all-out victory or in self-defence. In the long run, the benefits of aid must also be distributed so as to reduce the disparities between ethnic and religious groups, regions, or classes that fuel conflict. The complexity of this task is illustrated in the case of Cambodia, where donors' efforts to use conditionality to curtail illicit logging by armed groups were impeded by different views about how best to respond to the country's internal power struggles.

Chapter 3 zeroes in on fiscal policy, an area where the IFIs are particularly well-placed to reorient conditionality towards peace-related goals. A key issue is how to ensure that aid encourages domestic investment in peace programmes, rather than replacing it, since heavy reliance on external assistance is rarely sustainable over the long term. The contrasting experiences of El Salvador and neighbouring Guatemala suggest that the IFIs have overcome some of their earlier reluctance to address the politically sensitive issues of how to mobilise domestic revenues and shift public expenditures to support peace.

Chapter 4 explores the humanitarian dilemma that donors often face in war-torn societies, regardless of whether or not they apply conditionality. Aid that is meant to relieve suffering may prolong or re-ignite conflicts that are at the root of the suffering, particularly if there is much 'leakage' of aid to the belligerent parties. Yet imposing conditions can mean withholding aid from innocent civilians. Rather than making all aid conditional, donors could target selectively those types of assistance that are of most value to the political leaders and of least value to vulnerable populations.

The final chapter turns to the major obstacles to peace conditionality. Not all of these obstacles lie within the war-torn societies. On the donor side, competing governmental priorities and the internal dynamics of the aid agencies can pose serious constraints. For example, if donor governments put greater emphasis on winning commercial contracts than on securing peace, or if aid agencies gauge success in terms of money disbursed rather than results achieved, the scope for promoting a durable peace by means of conditional aid is circumscribed. Recipient governments, meanwhile, may claim that peace conditionality infringes on 'national sovereignty'. These obstacles must be faced squarely if conditionality is to become an effective instrument for building peace.

Chapter 1

Aid for Peace?

'Dayton,' former US Secretary of State Madeleine Albright once explained, 'was conceived as a bargain, between the international community on the one hand and the parties in Bosnia on the other.'[1] International aid has been a key element of this and other peace bargains. But just as the signing of an accord does not guarantee that peace will prevail, so the pledging of aid does not guarantee that external assistance will materialise. Wars can resume, as Angola has reminded us more than once; and today's promises of aid can be forgotten tomorrow.

When initial pledges of aid are premised on the signing of a peace accord, it seems logical to suppose that fulfillment of those pledges and the prospects for further aid would hinge upon steps by the recipients to implement the accord and consolidate peace. The linkages between aid and peace are seldom clearly defined, however, leaving donors and recipients with considerable room for manoeuvre. In principle, this flexibility could facilitate a smooth meshing between aid disbursements and efforts to build a lasting peace. In practice, however, it can result in a decoupling of the two. Peace conditionality seeks to address this problem by establishing closer links between the commitments of donors and recipients, in effect translating the 'grand bargain' of the peace accord into mini-bargains in which specific types and quantities of aid are tied to specific measures that are crucial to moving beyond conflict.

This chapter examines the potential for such mini-bargains as well as the limits of aid as a lever to influence recalcitrant parties. Both are illustrated by the experience gained in Bosnia since the signing of the Dayton Peace Agreement in December 1995.

Trial and error in Bosnia

Nowhere has the issue of leveraging aid for peace been more vigorously debated than in Bosnia. At the first international donor conference, held in Brussels a week after the signing of the Dayton accord, European Commissioner Hans van den Broek reaffirmed the official EU position that reconstruction aid to the former Yugoslavia should be conditional on the implementation of peace agreements, including respect for human rights, the right of refugees and displaced persons to return to their homes, and the surrender of indicted war criminals.[2] In April 1996, van den Broek and World Bank president James Wolfensohn co-chaired a second donors' conference, and jointly declared:

> *Developments on the ground should be constantly reviewed to ensure that aid is conditional on the thorough implementation of the obligations undertaken by all parties, in particular, full co-operation with the international tribunal for the prosecution of war criminals.*[3]

A dramatic display of donor resolve came in the Dayton agreement's first year. In the September 1996 elections held under Bosnia's new constitution, Momcilo Krajisnik, a close associate of indicted war criminal Radovan Karadzic, was elected as the Serb member of Bosnia's three-person collective presidency. In a gesture of continuing defiance toward the Dayton goal of a united Bosnia, Krajisnik then announced that he would refuse to attend the presidential swearing-in ceremony in Sarajevo, a move that threatened to undermine the fragile new state from its inception. Carl Bildt, the international community's High Representative in Bosnia, responded by sending his senior deputy for economic reconstruction to the Bosnian Serb leaders' headquarters in Pale, accompanied by the resident representatives of the World Bank, the European Bank for Reconstruction and Development, the EU, and US President Clinton's special envoy for reconstruction. Together they delivered a stern warning: not one penny of reconstruction aid would flow to Bosnia's Serb Republic if Krajisnik failed to appear. Four days later, he was in Sarajevo to attend the ceremony. The significance of this episode went beyond the modest victory of persuading a reluctant president to attend his own inauguration. It demonstrated that aid conditionality could furnish political muscle to a peace process, particularly when the donors take a united stance.

Bosnia also offers examples of some of the difficulties of using conditional aid as a policy tool. Around the same time that the international envoys visited Pale, another drama was unfolding in the city of Mostar in western Bosnia. During the war, the Bosnian Muslims (or Bosniacs) had been driven into east Mostar, while the Bosnian Croats took control of west Mostar, the two sides being separated by the Neretva River.[4] The EU assumed responsibility for Mostar's reconstruction shortly after the creation of Bosnia's Muslim–Croat Federation in 1994. As a precondition for rehabilitating the city's two main hydroelectric plants, the EU administrator insisted that the two sides must agree to share the electricity from both plants. Before such an agreement could be reached, however, the World Bank struck a unilateral deal with the Bosniacs to repair one of the power plants. The infuriated Croats then proceeded to repair the other, giving Mostar the dubious distinction of being the only city in the world with de facto apartheid in its electricity grid.

Elsewhere in Bosnia, donors have experimented by using aid as a lever to support the right of refugees and internally displaced persons to return to their homes. At the local level, the country's municipal authorities vary greatly in their commitment to Dayton's principles: some protected their minority residents during the war even at the risk of antagonising nationalist politicians; others led and profited personally from ethnic cleansing and now block minority returns; and many sit on the fence. In this setting, donors have an opportunity to allocate local aid selectively, so as to reward those seeking to implement the peace accord, penalise those who are obstructing its implementation, and encourage vacillators to get off the fence. A ministerial meeting of the Peace

Implementation Council endorsed this principle in May 1997, recommending that 'assistance for housing and local infrastructure should be dependent on the acceptance of return' of refugees and displaced persons.[5]

The office of the UN High Commissioner for Refugees (UN-HCR) pioneered this conditional aid strategy in its 'Open Cities' programme, targeting aid to municipalities whose officials publicly declare their willingness to welcome minority returns. Where public pronouncements are followed by actual minority returns, the agency provides reconstruction aid not only to the returnees but also to the majority community.[6] The UNHCR tailors the conditions for qualifying as an open city to local circumstances – in one municipality, the key issue may be processing the paperwork to return apartments to their former occupants, in another it may be school enrollment for minority children or the removal of wall posters inciting ethnic hatred. If local authorities renege on their commitments, open-city status and its attendant rewards can be rescinded. The programme has not always succeeded in enforcing these conditions, and the qualifying localities have not necessarily been the places to which displaced persons are most anxious to return. Despite these flaws, the UNHCR initiative offers valuable lessons that could inform similar experiments elsewhere.[7]

There is also scope for peace conditionality in donor relationships with the private sector. For example, the US Agency for International Development (USAID) requires banks and loan recipients in its private-sector lending programme in Bosnia to certify that none of their officers, directors, or principal shareholders has been indicted or is being investigated for war crimes. Similarly, banks must pledge not to discriminate against loan applicants on the basis of ethnicity or religion. The International Crisis Group (ICG) has proposed that donors go further to include a set of Minority Employment Principles in their contracts with Bosnian enterprises, akin to the Sullivan Principles for companies doing business in South Africa in the 1980s.[8] These would go beyond non-discrimination (which presupposes that minorities apply for jobs) to something more akin to affirmative action in US domestic policy. To qualify for contracts, businesses would be required to hire from minorities based on guidelines that take into account

such factors as the current and pre-war composition of the municipality's population and the amount of aid involved. In the first
year of a contract, for example, the company might be required to
hire 10% more from minorities than their current share in the local
population, with higher targets in succeeding years up to the
pre-war demographic balance – a policy that would aim to make
minority returnees an economic asset to local communities. This
proposal drew a cool response from a senior World Bank official,
who argued that private companies should base their hiring decisions on 'commercial grounds only' and that enforcing such requirements would be impractical. But the aid donors are not
investing in Bosnia on commercial grounds: they are investing to
build peace. And the fact that enforcement of rules is costly does
not mean that the optimal policy is no rules at all. Rather, decisions
as to whether to implement such principles should be made after
weighing the benefits to the peace process against the administrative costs.

Aid-for-peace bargains

As these examples from Bosnia illustrate, aid-for-peace bargains
face two basic stumbling blocks: the aid-for-peace offer first must
be *accepted*, and then *enforced*. Peace conditionality can be seen as a
response to the problem of enforcing the overarching bargain
represented by peace accords and the accompanying pledges of
aid, by proceeding through a series of more specific bargains.
These 'mini-bargains' disaggregate the acceptance and enforcement
problems into smaller and more tractable pieces, but do not elimin-
ate them altogether.

The acceptance problem

Acceptance of the aid-for-peace offer depends not only on its
terms, but also on the fallback positions of the contending parties
should they fail to reach an agreement with the donors. Alternative
sources of financial support – for example, from other external
backers who do not impose comparable conditions, or from the
profits of trading in commodities such as logs, gems, or drugs –
bolster the parties' fallback positions and reduce the leverage of aid
donors.[9] Erosion of these fallback positions can improve the

prospects for an aid-for-peace bargain. For example, when South Africa's government withdrew support from Mozambique's Renamo guerrillas, they became more willing to opt for peace.

Trade sanctions and the threat or use of force can alter fallback positions, making an aid-for-peace bargain more attractive, especially to 'opportunistic spoilers' whose aims expand or shrink depending on perceived benefits, costs and risks.[10] It is widely believed, for example, that trade and financial sanctions played a crucial role in persuading Serbian leader Slobodan Milosevic to accept the Dayton Peace Agreement.[11] The US government's suspension of trade preferences for Guatemala in 1993, in response to President Jorge Serrano's move to usurp constitutional rule, deepened the Guatemalan business sector's opposition to the coup and may have thereby contributed to its ultimate failure.[12] Moreover, 'smart' sanctions, such as asset freezes and travel restrictions, can target individual rulers, minimising human costs and risks of a political backlash in favour of the rulers, both of which often come with more generalised sanctions.[13]

While trade sanctions can be effective against legitimate exporters and importers, it is more difficult to curtail illicit trading by armed groups. In Cambodia, for example, the UN Transitional Authority's (UNTAC's) inability to prevent exports of logs and gems by the Khmer Rouge (KR) made aid ineffective in winning the KR's adherence to the Paris peace accord; in effect, their export earnings 'eliminated this bargaining chip'.[14] Similarly, in Angola the diamond trade that finances the National Union for the Total Independence of Angola (UNITA) guerrillas and the non-transparent oil revenues that finance the government have long undermined international efforts to broker an end to the conflict.[15] Recent initiatives have attempted to address these problems: in spring 2000, the UN Security Council moved to tighten sanctions on trade with the guerrillas, while the IMF concluded an agreement with the Angolan government to allow independent external auditors to monitor its oil revenues.[16]

In some settings, the stick of force can be a critical complement to the carrot of aid. For example, during the first year of the Dayton agreement, the Bosnia's Serb Republic received only 2% of the $900 million in reconstruction aid disbursed in the country, due to the refusal of its hardline leaders based in Pale to comply with key provisions of the accord. Meanwhile, external assistance to the armed forces of the Bosnian–Croat Federation shifted the country's military balance against the Serb Republic, and in the following year NATO-led forces arrested several indicted war criminals and seized police stations and television transmitters from the hardliners. The promise of aid and the threat of force together contributed to Serb Republic president Biljana Plavsic's decision to break from the Pale leaders in 1997 and to the election of a pro-Dayton prime minister in the Serb Republic in 1998.

The enforcement problem

The acceptance of an aid-for-peace bargain is only a first step in using aid to leverage a durable peace. The bargain must then be enforced. The enforcement problem surfaces clearly in a World Bank evaluation of aid to Cambodia after the Paris peace accord: the Cambodian authorities 'were quick to agree to virtually every idea presented by an agency bringing funds', the evaluation reports, but the country's co-prime ministers showed 'no respect for what they themselves sign', reflecting the belief that 'Cambodia can get money from the Bank with no strings attached'.[17] Donors can address the enforcement problem by employing one or more elements of a four-pronged strategy:

- *Monitoring compliance*: monitoring compliance with the aid-for-peace bargains is an unfamiliar task for aid agencies. Traditionally, many donors have measured success simply in terms of money disbursed, as if this were the end itself rather than a means to other objectives. Where performance has been evaluated in terms of outcomes, the usual measures are physical (for example, miles of roads built or repaired) or economic (e.g., the impact on growth or employment). After a civil war, these conventional measures need to be supplemented by evidence of progress in building peace. In some cases, aid donors may be able to monitor compliance with aid-for-peace bargains by tapping the expertise of other agencies, such as the Office of the High Representative in Bosnia or the UN Verification Missions in El Salvador and Guatemala. In other cases, however, they will need to invest time and money to develop their own in-house capacity.

- *Slicing the carrot*: the prospect of aid provides leverage but once the aid is delivered, the leverage it offers is largely dissipated. Thereafter, new leverage comes only from the prospect of further aid. To maintain leverage, donors can divide their aid into installments, or 'tranches', with the delivery of the next install-ment dependent on progress in meeting the terms set for the previous one. This has long been standard practice at the IMF, where loan disbursements are subject to increasingly strict macroeconomic policy conditions as the borrower draws on successive tranches. An alternative is the inclusion of a contrac-tual clause in aid agreements in which the recipient agrees to undertake a specific action by a specific date, with a provision for suspension of disbursements in the event of non-compliance. Such 'dated covenants' are often used by the World Bank and the regional development banks; for example, a transportation-sector loan may require the borrower to increase railway tariffs by a certain date. Both tranched assistance and dated covenants could be used in an analogous fashion to enforce aid-for-peace bargains.

- *Combating corruption*: since the end of the Cold War, aid donors have devoted greater attention to the adverse effects of corrup-tion on efficiency, investment, tax revenues, and growth.[18] In regions emerging from conflict, corruption gives political leaders easy access to money and other resources, thus enhancing their fallback positions and making it more difficult to enforce peace conditionality. The systematic diversion of revenues from the public treasury to private pockets and political organisations – via tax exemptions or the provision of other government favours in return for informal side-payments, off-the-books sales of pub-lic assets or products of public enterprises, and the extortion of informal 'taxes' from legitimate businesses – is not uncommon in the aftermath of civil wars. Donors are sometimes inclined to turn a blind eye to such practices, on the grounds that they sustain political patronage networks and help to grease the wheels of the peace process. In the end, however, corruption erodes donor leverage, in addition to the corrosive effects it has on the economy. The long-run benefits of a resolute stand against corruption are likely to outweigh the short-term political costs.

- *Inter-donor coordination*: finally, effective enforcement of aid-for-peace bargains requires coordination among donors. This can be difficult, not only because agencies may differ in their priorities, but also because they protect their own autonomy and often compete for projects with high visibility or 'flagpole value'. Yet in the absence of inter-donor coordination, aid recipients can be expected to shop around for offers of assistance with a minimum of strings attached, driving the aid-for-peace bargain to the lowest common denominator. The Mostar hydroelectric power episode recounted above illustrates this risk.

This chapter has characterised peace conditionality as a bargain between aid donors and recipients. The examples from Bosnia and the discussion of acceptance and enforcement problems expose some of the problems that donors face in using aid as a lever to secure a lasting peace. The next chapter examines further the complexities that arise from the fact that aid flows not to the recipient country as a whole, but rather to contending individuals, groups and classes within the country. An analysis of how external assistance affects the balances of power among these internal political forces is particularly crucial in the case of aid after a civil war.

Chapter 2

The Internal Politics of External Assistance

The struggle for power that drives civil wars enters a new phase with the signing of a peace accord. If negotiated endings to civil wars are 'most likely in situations in which opponents are roughly equal in terms of power, resources and goals' – a balance that discourages either side from pursuing outright victory – a similar logic applies to their implementation.[1] If the balance of power shifts so sharply as to tempt one side to renew the quest for a military solution, or the other to return to arms in self-defence, the tenuous movement towards peace can quickly falter.

This chapter explores the impact of external assistance on internal balances of power in war-torn societies. In principle, well-targeted aid can strengthen the internal forces that are committed to a peaceful resolution of conflict. But poorly targeted aid can have the opposite effect, increasing the influence of 'spoilers' and tilting the power balance against a negotiated settlement. A central aim of peace conditionality is to ensure that external assistance reinforces the internal political foundations for building peace.

The intersection of economics and politics

The need to consider the political effects of assistance is important since aid does not flow to countries in the abstract, but rather to specific groups and individuals. In so doing, aid inexorably affects the relative influence of different parties within the recipient country. This happens regardless of whether or not conditions are attached to the aid, as Peter Uvin observes in an illuminating account of aid to Rwanda prior to the 1994 genocide:

> [P]olitical conditionality was never really implemented in Rwanda; there were few credible threats and even less action to diminish Rwanda's financial lifeline. After all, we should not forget that aid to Rwanda greatly increased during the period. ... In so doing, the aid system sent a message ... and it essentially said that, on the level of practice and not discourse, the aid system did not care unduly about political and social trends in the country, not even if they involved government-sponsored racist attacks against Tutsi. ... The problem is that we tend to conceptualize our choices as between negative conditionality and the continuation of business as usual. The former is clearly an action fraught with risks and uncertainties, while the latter is perceived to be neutral – amounting to no action at all. That is wrong: the continuation of business as usual is a form of action, it does send signals, and it has an impact on local political and social processes.[2]

Yet donors often turn a blind eye to the political impacts of their aid, or at least profess blindness. World Bank officials, for example, often invoke their mandate to make loans 'with due attention to considerations of economy and efficiency and without regard to political or other non-economic influences or considerations'.[3] Assessing the impact of World Bank and IMF aid to Rwanda, a 1999 report of the UK Parliament points out the political consequences of this ostensibly apolitical stance:

> As two of the most powerful international institutions in contact with the Rwandan Government, their concerns if expressed early enough might have proved important interventions. Neither organisation recognised the direct link between growing social tension, human rights abuses and the subsequent destruction of the entire economic infrastructure.[4]

In practice, 'economy and efficiency' seldom can be neatly divorced from 'political considerations'. The two spheres intersect and nowhere is this intersection larger than in countries torn by civil war. Given this overlap, the exclusionary clause in the World Bank's charter can be read in two different ways: either as excluding all political considerations regardless of their economic importance, or as ruling out only those political considerations that are economically irrelevant. The overwhelming economic impacts of war and peace clearly expose the absurdity of the first reading.

Aid and power in Cambodia

Cambodia's experience vividly illustrates both the political weight of external assistance and the potential for aid conditionality to help ensure that this weight does not tilt internal power balances toward the resumption of war. The 1991 Paris Peace Agreement was signed by Cambodia's three main warring parties: the Cambodian People's Party (CPP), who had governed most of the country since the 1979 Vietnamese invasion, despite a crippling Western aid and trade embargo; the Khmer Rouge (KR), during whose rule from 1975 to 1979 more than one million Cambodians died from executions, hunger, and disease; and the United National Front for an Independent, Neutral, Peaceful, and Cooperative Cambodia (Funcinpec), a royalist party led by Prince Norodom Sihanouk and his son, Prince Ranariddh, who fought against the Vietnamese-backed government in the 1980s in alliance with the KR.

Following the Paris agreement, UNTAC, the most ambitious peacekeeping operation the UN had ever mounted, oversaw preparations for the May 1993 elections and administered the country until the newly elected government took power later that year. During the UNTAC period, nominal sovereignty was vested in the Supreme National Council (SNC), which comprised the Cambodian signatories to the accords. But much of the country's *de facto* administration remained in the hands of the CPP, the only party with the cadres to carry out the day-to-day functions of government.

While the CPP and Funcinpec carried their contest for power into the electoral arena, the KR defected from the peace process in mid-1992 and took control of Cambodian territory along the Thai border. The KR saw the return to war as a viable fallback option, due above all to their ability to export logs and gems from the areas under their control. This trade, which relied on the complicity of elements of the Thai military, brought the KR about $20m per month in late 1992. International pressure to curtail this illicit traffic initially met with limited success at best.[5]

Meanwhile, the UNTAC operation brought an unprecedented influx of external resources into Cambodia. UNTAC's $1.5bn budget included not only salaries for more than 15,000 peacekeeping troops and 7,000 civilian UN personnel (whose daily allowances were roughly equal to the annual income of an average Cambodian), but also salary support for Cambodian soldiers and civil servants, dubbed 'Operation Paymaster'.[6] This expenditure sparked a 'construction and services boomlet', particularly in the capital, Phnom Penh. In the words of a World Bank report, 'The transition to a market economy was underway.'[7]

External assistance for rehabilitation and reconstruction began at the same time, with initial aid disbursements of $250m in 1992 and over $300m in 1993.[8] Concerns about the prospective political fallout from these disbursements triggered manoeuvres among both donors and recipients. Some bilateral donors, worried that aid would disproportionately strengthen the CPP if channeled through the SNC-led state, worked only through non-governmental organisations. The IFIs could not bypass the SNC, however, since it was 'the only body with the authority to re-establish Cambodia's membership in good standing and commit the country to debt obligations'.[9] At the same time, the Cambodian parties jockeyed not only to capture aid but also to limit aid to their adversaries. Within the SNC, for example, Funcinpec managed to block a $75m budget support loan from the World Bank, fearing that it would confer an electoral advantage on the CPP.[10]

Funcinpec won a plurality in the May 1993 elections, securing 45% of the vote. The CPP, which was placed second with 38%, refused to accept the result and threatened secession in the country's eastern provinces. At a meeting in the royal palace in June, the Core Group of nations that had sponsored the Paris agreement played the peace-conditionality card by insisting that further aid to

Cambodia was contingent on all parties accepting the election results, which had been endorsed by the UN Security Council.[11] A power-sharing compromise was reached, the centerpiece of which was a novel arrangement in which Funcipec's Prince Ranariddh and the CPP's Hun Sen became co-prime ministers. Ministerial portfolios were divided among the parties, pairing ministers from one side with deputy ministers from the other. The compromise reflected the delicate balance of forces between Funcinpec's electoral edge, fortified by international pressure, and the CPP's on-the-ground administrative and military superiority.

With the formation of a new government, the power struggle between the CPP and Funcinpec 'moved inside the cabinet and the bureaucracy'.[12] The civil service, already regarded as bloated by the IMF and World Bank, grew further to accommodate backers of Funcinpec and smaller coalition parties. The continuing low-level war against the KR provided a reason, or at least a pretext, to maintain the size of the military, composed of rival forces loyal to the CPP and Funcinpec. The two coalition partners proceeded to compete for logging concessions, kickbacks on government contracts, and most destabilising of all, the allegiance of defecting KR leaders and troops.

This context was not terribly conducive to public or private investment. A World Bank evaluation reported delays in implementing a number of projects because of mutual 'distrust or rent-seeking power struggles between officials of the rival parties in the coalition'.[13] Private investment did not fare much better. Apart from the boom in urban construction, and some low-cost investments in garment factories to take advantage of international quotas, private investment largely failed to take off. The country is not attracting the 'right investors', a World Bank official complained in 1997, 'only those who want to operate in this murky situation.'[14]

The sharpest expression of donor disquiet came from the IMF, which had approved a $120m loan in 1994 to be disbursed in six semi-annual installments. After repeated delays and freezes of the loan disbursements due to the Cambodian government's failure to meet performance targets, IMF representative Hubert Neiss, speaking at a July 1997 meeting in Paris of the donors' Consultative Group (CG) for Cambodia, delivered a remarkably candid appraisal of the magnitude of official corruption. By 'conservative' calculations, he reported:

> *Overall, the diversion of public resources has probably reached the same amount as actual budget revenue collections, or nearly 10 percent of GDP. Obviously, this trend has to be reversed to save the country's economy from serious damage. Such damage simply cannot be ignored by IFIs and donors who must take a longer-term view on economic viability.*[15]

Neiss estimated that illegal logging alone was responsible for 'well over $100m' in lost revenues in the previous year, and declared that this was the 'single most critical issue in Cambodia'. He therefore announced that IMF aid would be resumed only when credible steps were taken to halt illegal logging and to bring the proceeds of forest exploitation into the government budget.

In an unusual step, signaling the gravity of the donors' concerns, the World Bank, as chair of the Consultative Group, immediately faxed a letter directly to Cambodia's two prime ministers summarising the Paris discussions. After recounting the donors' concerns about inadequate revenue collection, uncontrolled logging and the lack of transparency and accountability, the letter made it clear that the disbursement of the $450m in new aid pledges elicited at the meeting would be conditional on 'firm and timely steps' to remedy these problems.[16]

Tensions within the CPP-Funcinpec coalition had mounted in the preceding months, occasionally flaring into violence as the two sides competed to attract defectors from the disintegrating KR. Shortly after the Paris meeting, full-scale fighting erupted in Phnom Penh. Some 150 people, including several top Funcinpec commanders, were killed, and Prince Ranariddh fled to Thailand.

The donors' response to this violent dissolution of the coalition government was mixed. The US government suspended all new aid and terminated several existing programmes, over the objections of local embassy staff. The Japanese government, Cambodia's biggest aid donor, adopted a less confrontational public posture, stating that its assistance would continue if the existing constitutional framework was maintained and 'free and fair' elections were held in 1998. In the meantime, major Japanese-financed infrastructure projects were stalled in the pipeline, ostensibly due to the deteriorated security situation: 'We said, "We can't send our engineers",' a Japanese official explained, 'but we're very sure that he [Hun Sen] understood the real reasons.'[17] Other donors, including the World Bank and the Asian Development Bank, continued existing projects but quietly put new assistance on hold, pending a political solution that would restore a semblance of democratic rule.

A Japanese-brokered agreement led to national elections in July 1998, in which the CPP won a majority of seats in the national assembly but fewer than the two-thirds needed to form a new government. After protracted negotiations, Funcinpec agreed to join the CPP in a new coalition government, with Hun Sen as the sole Prime Minister and Ranariddh as chairman of the national assembly. Former finance minister Sam Rainsy, who had founded his own party, became leader of the opposition.

In response to this political accommodation, the donors convened another CG meeting in February 1999 and pledged $470m of fresh aid to Cambodia. Seeking to tie disbursements more closely to progress in such key areas as forestry management and military demobilisation, the donors arranged to meet with the government every three months to monitor progress. The IMF agreed to a new, three-year, $80m loan in October 1999. International pressure to crack down on illegal logging continued, and at the end of 2001 Hun Sen announced a suspension of all logging operations. In the country's first-ever local elections, held in February 2002 amid sporadic violence, the CPP retained control of most communes, but the introduction of multi-party councils with proportional representation brought new checks and balances to local government.

It would be premature to conclude that Cambodia has completed the transition from war to peace. The threat of violent conflict has receded, but not disappeared. But as documented above, aid conditionality has played an important role in the advances made thus far. During the UNTAC period, aid helped to maintain the balance of power between the CPP and Funcinpec, despite the KR's abandonment of the peace agreement. After the 1993 elections, the Core Group of donor governments used conditionality to bring the CPP into a coalition government. When the coalition collapsed and violence broke out in 1997, aid conditionality again helped to pave the way for new elections and a return to coalition rule in 1998.

A key challenge remains the creation of a transparent and equitable system of revenue collection – an issue explored further in the next chapter – both to secure a sustainable financial base for government and to curb the flow of illicit funds to private armies. Here too, aid donors led by the IMF have sought to apply conditionality, spurred by the efforts of non-governmental organisations to expose the extent of illegal logging.[18] While progress on this front has been slow, it may have been non-existent but for aid conditionality.

Striking the balance

It is a truism that political change must originate from within a country, and cannot be imposed from the outside. If no domestic forces backed peace accord implementation, there would be little scope for effective peace conditionality. On the other hand, if there were an overwhelming national consensus in favour of implementing the accords, there would be little need for it. After a negotiated ending to a civil war, most countries lie in the intermediate terrain between these poles, with domestic opinion divided between supporters of the accords and the hardliners on one or more sides who would prefer a return to armed conflict over implementation of the accords. In such settings, peace conditionality can play a useful role.

Critics of the efforts of aid donors to promote democratisation and the rule of law have stressed that 'outside aid is no substitute for the will to reform'.[19] Yet in the wake of a civil war, reform is seldom a simple matter of 'political will' or the lack of it. Instead it involves a clash of wills: some people want to implement peace-related reforms, while others do not. Donors should not assume naively that everyone in the country favours the faithful implementation of the peace accords, but neither should they assume that the alignment of domestic forces is immutable or beyond their influence.

As the Cambodian case illustrates, peace conditionality can affect the balance of power within war-torn societies. But at the same time, the balance of power affects the scope for peace conditionality, too. The greater the parity among the contending domestic parties, the stronger the bargaining position of the aid donors. When one party wields disproportionate power, the donors are less able to exercise leverage on the strong and less willing to exercise it on the weak. Similarly, when one party threatens to act as a spoiler, the donors often are less willing to exercise leverage on the more cooperative players. As long as the KR threat persisted in Cambodia, for example, many donors hesitated to press too hard on the CPP and Funcinpec to demobilise their armed forces or to tackle related issues such as illicit logging.

Both the need for peace conditionality and the scope to exercise it can change over time, as the balance of power shifts among domestic political forces. In the year following the Dayton Peace Agreement, for example, the donors largely withheld reconstruction aid from Bosnia's Serb Republic, worried that aid would bolster the power of hardliners opposed to implementation of the agreement. This danger was underscored in a Human Rights Watch report documenting how British aid in the town of Prijedor in the Serb Republic was controlled by local strongmen who had led 'ethnic cleansing' operations during the war.[20] Despite the fact that their reconstruction plan originally earmarked 27.5% of the aid for the Serb Republic, the donors channeled 98% to the Bosnian–Croat Federation.

After a year, the international community's High Representative in Bosnia, Carl Bildt, suggested that the donors had failed to strike the right balance. 'Frankly, conditionality hasn't been working on either side,' he complained. 'The Federation is convinced money will flow to it no matter what, and Republika Srpska [the Serb Republic] is convinced it won't receive aid under any circumstances.'[21] In the next year the flow of reconstruction funds to the Serb Republic increased to about 10% of the total. This taste of the aid carrot – coupled with other pressures, including military aid to the Federation army, as discussed in the previous chapter –

encouraged the emergence of more moderate Bosnian–Serb leaders, and in the next two years, the Serb Republic's share of Bosnian reconstruction aid rose to 27%.[22]

The emergence of pro-Dayton leaders in the Serb Republic enabled the donors to adopt a less compliant stance vis-à-vis hardliners on the Federation side. The successful US-led move in 1997 to block IMF and World Bank loans to Croatia until its government surrendered ten Bosnian–Croat war-crimes suspects to The Hague tribunal was one dramatic signal of this shift. At the same time, the donors voiced 'disappointment' at the failure of Federation authorities to facilitate minority returns to Sarajevo, the Bosnian capital, and in February 1998 they moved formally to make further reconstruction aid to the city conditional on meeting specific targets for minority returns.[23] When these targets were not met in subsequent months, the US suspended roughly $5m of aid. Peace conditionality in Bosnia thus became a two-way street, applied to aid to the Federation as well as the Serb Republic.

The political dynamics of countries embarked on the perilous transition from war to peace compel aid donors to think not only in terms of assisting the country as a whole, but also in terms of assisting specific individuals, groups and classes within the country. The issues of who receives aid, and what conditions are attached to that aid, are seldom unimportant, but in war-torn societies they acquire a special urgency. 'If you are designing a project for a seismic zone,' a member of the World Bank staff remarked, 'you need to take account of the risk of earthquakes.'[24] This logic applies equally well to the 'social seismic zones' of countries with a recent history of violent conflict.

This implies the need for departures from business-as-usual, both in the appraisal of aid projects and in the formulation of economic policy recommendations for recipient governments. In project appraisal, the conventional tool used by donor agencies is cost-benefit analysis, in which the monetary values of benefits and costs are added up, and the project deemed worthy if the former exceeds the latter. In this calculation, distributional concerns are brushed aside; it does not matter who gets benefits and who bears costs. This approach is disingenuous in the best of circumstances, but in conflict-prone societies it is foolhardy. A single-minded focus on how to make a bigger pie is not 'efficient' when conflicts over its division threaten to smash the pie. Instead of weighing all the benefits and costs of the project equally, regardless of to whom they accrue, donors need to evaluate how they are distributed. One way to do so is to put greater weight on benefits (and costs) to some groups than to others, for example, by counting dollars as being worth more to the poor than to the rich. Methodologies for this purpose are well-known, but rarely applied in practice.[25] Another potentially useful decision-making tool is conflict impact assessment to analyse how aid projects will affect the cleavages of class, ethnicity and region that form the fault lines of violent conflict.[26] Like the environmental impact assessments introduced in most aid agencies in the past two decades, these assessments must proceed through a learning curve. Yet however imperfect, some assessment is likely to be better than none at all.[27]

Similar conclusions apply to the aid donors' economic policy recommendations – the main arena in which conditionality has been practised in the past, particularly by the IFIs. Again, 'economy and efficiency' cannot be divorced from political considerations: the size of tomorrow's pie may depend on how it is sliced today. This has major implications for fiscal policy, the topic of the next chapter.

Chapter 3

Peace Dividends: Aid and Fiscal Policy

If aid donors are willing to foot the bill, why should a recipient government mobilise domestic resources to finance peace implementation? Why bear the political costs of raising taxes or reallocating public expenditure, when external resources can be tapped for peace-related needs? This incentive problem arises even if the programmes mandated by the peace accords are embraced wholeheartedly by the ruling party. It is compounded if some of these programmes are accepted only grudgingly, being seen as concessions to the other side.

Aid donors face a dilemma. Their money can play a crucial role in helping to support the implementation of peace accords and the consolidation of a durable peace. Yet at the same time, their aid can also perpetuate the very shortfalls in domestic funding that it seeks to compensate. In the long run, peace-related programmes – from establishing new democratic institutions to promoting greater public spending on health and education – will be sustainable only if they are financed domestically.

Conditionality can help to counter the tendency for aid to discourage or 'crowd out' local investment. By linking aid to fiscal commitments by the recipient government, donors can encourage or 'crowd in' local funding for the costs of peace. The aim is to ensure that external resources complement rather than substitute for internal resources.

The need for policies to secure an internal 'peace dividend' emerged as a major issue in both El Salvador and Guatemala in the wake of their negotiated peace accords in the 1990s. In El Salvador, the failure of the IFIs to press the government to mobilise domestic resources to fund its commitments under the peace accords prompted sharp criticism from the UN. In neighboring Guatemala, where explicit fiscal targets were included in the accords, the UN and the IFIs worked together more closely. This chapter reviews these experiences, and draws lessons for fiscal policy and conditionality after civil wars.

Paying for peace in El Salvador

In March 1992, international donors convened in Washington DC to pledge support for El Salvador's peace process. Speaking for the Salvadoran government, which two months earlier had signed a peace accord with left-wing insurgents, Planning Minister Mirna Liévano de Marques reported on an analysis of the economic implications of the peace accord that had been undertaken by the government with IMF and World Bank support: 'Given the country's fiscal and financial realities, the possibilities for internal finance of the [National Reconstruction Plan] are extremely limited, hence we require substantial assistance from the international community.'[1] The World Bank, which chaired the meeting, emphasised that 'the reconstruction effort would not be used as a pretext for abandoning disciplined macroeconomic policy'.[2] In the words of one US official, the stance of the Salvadoran government was, 'If you [donors] want it to happen, you pay for it.'[3] The donors responded by pledging $800m in aid.

One year later, the donors reconvened in Paris. The World Bank's representative reiterated that 'adequate external financial support to finance priority peace-related expenditures is the critical condition for the consolidation of peace and social progress'.[4] Other donors, however, expressed unease about the government's failure to mobilise greater domestic resources for peace programmes. In a joint statement, the representatives of the Nordic countries warned that programmes for the establishment of democratic institutions and the transfer of land to ex-combatants 'remain dangerously underfunded' and called on the government 'to increase its own efforts to finance the peace process out of its own revenue'. Noting that El Salvador's ratio of tax revenue to gross domestic product (GDP) was less than 9% – among the lowest in the world – the Nordic statement pointedly remarked: 'If taxpayers in the donor countries make additional support to El Salvador possible, then it is only fair to expect that some extraordinary efforts are made to increase tax revenue within El Salvador.'[5]

The government's tax effort was not the only symptom of its lukewarm commitment to meeting the fiscal requirements of implementing the peace accords. Another telling indicator was its reluctance to redirect public expenditure to 'high-priority' peace programmes. Military spending, for example, continued to absorb more than twice its pre-war fraction of national income, notwithstanding the end of the war: the defence budget absorbed 2.2% of GDP in 1992 and 1.7% in 1993, compared to 0.7% before the war.[6] Meanwhile, the government reported to the donors in Paris that available funds (including government resources and amounts already pledged by donors) for the land transfer programme for ex-combatants amounted to only 50% of estimated needs; funds for democratic institutions – the newly created human-rights ombudsman's office, the elections tribunal, and judicial reform – covered only 74% of their requirements; and funds for the national civilian police, mandated by the peace accords to replace war-time paramilitary forces, amounted to a scant 24% of the estimated cost.[7]

Yet the World Bank and the IMF, the two donors with the greatest ability to influence the government's fiscal policies, avoided the issue of mobilising domestic resources to finance the costs of peace. Instead they colluded in the government's effort to shift the burden to the donors in the name of 'macroeconomic discipline'. In the words of Alvaro de Soto, who brokered the Salvadoran peace accord on behalf of the UN, the World Bank and the IMF 'followed their perceived path as if there were no war'.[8]

The failure of the IFIs to apply peace conditionality to fiscal policy slowed the pace of El Salvador's adjustment toward peace, but did not fatally compromise these efforts. The land transfer programme for ex-combatants ultimately transferred about 10% of the country's agricultural land to some 35,000 families, with funding provided mainly by the US.[9] This achievement was dampened, however, by low and declining real prices for agriculture and by inequitable access to technical assistance, infrastructure, inputs, and credit, which imperiled the programme's economic viability.[10] The National Civilian Police (PNC) eventually was fully deployed, and funded largely by the Salvadoran government itself, in response to growing public alarm over a post-war crime wave and revelations of the involvement of senior officers of the old national police in organised crime. Yet in the meantime violent crime had escalated to a point where homicide rates rivaled death-squad killings during the war, with San Salvador's central morgue handling 300 corpses per month.[11]

As a proportion of national income, El Salvador's public spending on education and health remains the second lowest in Latin America, next to that of Guatemala.[12] An internal evaluation of the World Bank's post-war lending in El Salvador notes that 'public revenues remain among the lowest in Latin America due to low tax rates, a narrow base, and high evasion' and reports that some Bank staff members now concede that 'the Bretton Woods institutions could have pushed harder at the outset on tax effort'.[13] On the question of conditionality, the evaluation observes:

> [T]he relatively low ratios of tax revenues and health and education expenditures to GDP, and relatively high ratio of military expenditures to GDP, compared to other Central American countries, does lend weight to the argument that the Bank and Fund could have pursued domestic resource mobilization and expenditure reallocation more aggressively than they have. … [I]f tax effort and the pattern of public expenditures have a direct bearing on post-conflict reconstruction, as they did in El Salvador, it is legitimate to include these parameters in the conditionality agenda.[14]

Fiscal targets in the Guatemalan peace accords

The fiscal stumbling blocks on the road to peace in El Salvador were very much on the minds of the peace negotiators in neighbouring Guatemala as they forged the series of agreements that culminated in the Accord for a Firm and Lasting Peace signed in December 1996. A key lesson drawn from the Salvadoran experience by UN mediator Jean Arnault was the need to engage the IFIs in the negotiation process. To this end, he invited representatives from the World Bank and Inter-American Development Bank (IDB) to participate in the protracted negotiations that led to the May 1996 socioeconomic accord.[15] IFI officials met with government negotiators in Washington and with Guatemalan National Revolutionary Unity (URNG) negotiators in Mexico City; the IDB designated a staff member to provide technical support for the negotiations; and a World Bank official worked closely with Arnault in drafting the agreement. These institutional and personal contacts laid the basis for continuing IFI engagement after the signing of the accords – a marked departure from the curtain between the IFIs' lending policies and the requirements of the peace process in El Salvador.[16]

Ironically, donor fatigue also helped to spur closer attention to the fiscal requirements of peacebuilding. 'Guatemala benefited from the perception in mid-1990s that the world was no longer interested in Central American conflicts, so Guatemala could not expect much help from the international community,' Arnault recalls. 'Therefore much attention was given to the mobilisation of domestic resources, especially to the tax issue.'[17] The socioeconomic accord committed the government to increasing tax revenues from 8% of national income (the second lowest level in the western hemisphere, next to Haiti) to 12% within four years, and specified that the tax system shall be 'fair, equitable and, on the whole, progressive'.[18] The accord also mandated 50% increases in the share of national income devoted to public spending on health and education, and a 50% reduction in the share devoted to the military.

Meeting these commitments would be no small achievement. Guatemala's tax ratio averaged 7.9% in the preceding 36 years, never surpassing 10.2%, testimony to the deep antipathy of the country's ruling elite to taxation for social spending.[19] Yet by Latin American standards the tax and expenditure targets are modest; health and education spending as a fraction of national income, for example, still would be only one-third of the level in Costa Rica.

Visiting Guatemala in May 1997, IMF Managing Director Michel Camdessus declared that the key condition for concluding a stand-by agreement with the Fund was compliance with the fiscal commitments that the government had already accepted in the peace accords. Regarding the tax-ratio target, Camdessus remarked that the IMF would have preferred a more ambitious target of at least 14% and cautioned that without a significant increase in the tax effort, the country could not expect to receive substantial international aid. In contrast to its earlier stance in El Salvador, the World Bank also tied its aid to the implementation of the peace accords, offering to lend $310m to Guatemala but warning that 'we would be prepared to lower our lending to about $200m if the government were no longer making progress along the lines of the peace accords, in particular the socioeconomic accord'.[20]

Despite international encouragement, progress has been slow. By the year 2000, four years after the peace accords took effect, Guatemala's tax-to-GDP ratio had reached only 9.4%, well short of the 12% target. The inter-party commission charged with monitoring the implementation of the peace accords deferred the deadline for meeting the target to 2002. In an effort to forge a domestic political consensus on how to increase tax revenues, a broad-based commission, the 'Fiscal Pact for a Future with Peace and Development' was created, in a break with the historic taboo on public discussion of fiscal policy in Guatemala.[21]

In November 2001, acknowledging delays in compliance with a number of commitments under the peace accords, the Guatemalan government's peace secretariat stressed the importance of fiscal constraints: '*the main problem has to do with the State's limited financial capacity*, because most of the pending commitments require financial resources that are not available to undertake them'.[22] This lack of resources in turn can be traced, in no small measure, to the discrepancy between the principle of progressive taxation endorsed in the peace accords and the actual distribution of the tax burden in Guatemala. For all but the top 10% of Guatemalans, the country's tax system is progressive; that is, taxes as a percentage of income rise with household incomes. But the top 10% of households – the richest Guatemalans – pay a lower rate than the middle-class households who comprise the next 30% of the country's income distribution.[23] Owing to the extreme inequality of incomes in Guatemala, the top 10% receive roughly half the national income.[24] Were the progressivity of the tax system carried into this tier, these households would pay about 17% of their income in taxes rather than the current 13%. The difference is roughly what would be needed to make up the shortfall between the tax target of the peace accords and current performance.

Tax policy in developing countries often faces a trade-off in tax policy between progressivity and administrative feasibility: indirect taxes such as the value-added tax are relatively easy to administer but tend to be regressive in their distributional impact, while direct taxes on income and property are progressive but harder to collect. One way out of this dilemma lies in the indirect taxation of luxury consumption. The richest 10% of Guatemalans spend roughly one-third of their incomes on imported luxury goods such as automobiles, electrical appliances, jewelry, and private airplanes.[25] A 30% tariff on these items would generate revenues equivalent to 5% of national income, raising total taxes well above the target set in the peace accords. Yet for ideological reasons, the IFIs have not advocated such taxes. The conventional wisdom among economists at the World Bank and IMF is that tariffs foster inefficiency by shielding domestic industries from the bracing effects of foreign competition. In Guatemala, however, as in many developing countries, there is no domestic automobile or aircraft industry to protect, making this argument irrelevant.

The problems in financing the implementation of the peace accords in El Salvador and Guatemala have prompted growing recognition of the need to rethink fiscal policy in light of the distinctive needs of countries emerging from civil war. In the short run, external assistance can help to fund postwar reconstruction, but in the long run, domestic resources must be mobilised to finance the new democratic institutions and development pro- grammes that are needed to consolidate a lasting peace. This means greater attention to the level of government revenue, the composition of public expenditure, and the distributional impact of fiscal policy. Building on the Salvadoran and Guatemalan experi- ences, the final section of this chapter explores these issues.

Fiscal policies for building peace

Donors, particularly the IFIs, often insist on fiscal policy reforms as a condition for aid. Their main objective in most cases is to curtail government budget deficits so as to foster macroeconomic stability. Yet this is not the only aspect of fiscal policy where conditionality can play a useful role, nor is it necessarily the most important. In addition to the size of the budget deficit, other issues include the total size of revenue and expenditure, government priorities for public spending, and the impacts of taxation and expenditure on the distribution of income. In the aftermath of a civil war, these issues often take on a special importance. This section considers each of these in turn, starting with the traditional priority of the IFIs, the government budget deficit.

Budget deficit reduction

Attempts to build a durable peace often require fiscal measures that fly in the face of conventional IFI policies. For example, the IMF, in its pursuit of the objective of macroeconomic stabilisation, often requires the borrower government to cut its budget deficit to specified percentages of GDP before successive installments of an IMF loan can be disbursed. Whatever the wisdom of these deficit-reduction targets – itself often a matter of debate – in regions emerging from civil war, their feasibility and desirability must be viewed through the distinctive lens of the requirements of establishing a viable peace. Insofar as the IMF's usual macroeconomic prescriptions clash with the aim of building peace, there is a compelling case for rethinking those prescriptions.

The need to rethink conventional wisdom emerged quite clearly during the early years of Cambodia's reconstruction efforts. Following the initial period of UN administration, the IMF and World Bank pressed the country's new coalition government to downsize the civil service by 20%. A senior UN official explains:

> *The IMF just applied its standard ratio: your population is 11 million people, so the size of your civil service should be x. But the historical circumstances here are almost unique. In 1979 Cambodia was a wasteland. It had no civil service, no banking, no money. Ninety per cent of the intelligentsia was dead. The new government put together a system, starting from nothing. They paid people in rice to teach. The fact that these people were not trained teachers is not their*

fault. You can't tell them now, 'You're useless,' and throw
them on the scrap heap. It's not decent, and it's not possible
politically.[26]

Instead of cutting public employment, the coalition government expanded it by about 15% to accommodate jobseekers from the erstwhile opposition. In an effort to appease the donors, the government trimmed the budget deficit by cutting non-salary expenditures. 'The outcome was "remarkable progress" on the macroeconomic balances,' a subsequent World Bank evaluation dryly observed, 'combined with continued erosion of non-maintained infrastructure and of health, education and other services.'[27]

Similar tensions between fiscal austerity and reconstruction efforts arose in post-war Mozambique. Asserting that macroeconomic stabilisation was an 'absolute prerequisite', the IMF pressed in 1995 for spending cuts and a rollback in a scheduled increase in the minimum wage. Fearing that these moves would jeopardise the long-term goals of economic recovery and political stabilisation, the ambassadors of the US, the Netherlands and Canada, and the resident representatives of the EU, United Nations Development Programme (UNDP), Finland and Switzerland, took the unusual step of writing a joint letter to the Fund to voice their concerns.[28] In the end, a compromise was hammered out: the spending cutbacks were slowed and the minimum wage increase remained in place.

Proponents of macroeconomic discipline argue, quite rightly, that rampant inflation can undermine political stability as well as economic recovery, and that inflation often hits especially hard at the real incomes of the poor. These are good reasons to control inflation by means of fiscal and monetary discipline. But policymakers do not face an all-or-nothing choice between hyperinflation and draconian austerity: fiscal and monetary stringency is invariably a matter of degree. It is true that beyond a certain point, profligate spending and soaring deficits could trigger rapid inflation and spark economic distress and political unrest. In the range between moderate deficits and none at all, however, a tradeoff often exists between the size of the deficit on the one hand and the social tensions generated by inadequate public expenditure on the other. Within this intermediate zone, higher government budget deficits can reduce social tensions by financing peace-related expenditures.[29] For this reason, the IFIs may need to forego doctrinaire insistence on deficit reduction in the aftermath of a civil war.

The level of revenue and expenditure

In principle, budget deficits can be reduced either by cutting expenditures or by raising revenues. In practice, the IFIs often press for expenditure cuts, devoting less attention to the level of expenditure and revenue at which fiscal balance is sought. In so doing, they are driven partly by expediency – cutting expenditure is often assumed to be easier than raising revenue – and partly by an ideological predilection for downsizing the public sector. Yet countries emerging from civil wars often have extremely low levels of both revenue and expenditure. El Salvador and Guatemala have the lowest levels of tax revenue and public expenditure, as a fraction of national income, in all of Latin America; Cambodia has the lowest levels in east and South-east Asia; and Bosnia appears to have the lowest levels in Europe.[30] In such contexts, expenditure reduction is not what is needed. Instead, raising revenues is crucial, both to avoid excessive deficits and to build a sustainable fiscal base for peace.

For one-time expenditures such as the repair of war-damaged infrastructure, external assistance can provide a feasible alternative to domestic resource mobilisation. But building peace also requires substantial continuing expenditures for new democratic institutions and social programmes. In addition, monies will be needed to operate and maintain the rebuilt infrastructure and to repay loans for reconstruction. In the long run, raising domestic revenue is the only way to finance these costs.

From an administrative standpoint, one of the easiest ways to collect taxes is through tariffs on imports. Apart from raising revenues for the government, tariffs can also help to protect domestic industries that are struggling to recover from the effects of war. Despite the historic importance of tariff revenues in the now-industrialised countries – in the US, for example, customs duties accounted for roughly half of federal government revenue in 1900 [31] – today the IFIs are ideologically committed to lowering tariffs in developing countries in the name of trade liberalisation. The benefits of freer trade, however, must be weighed carefully against the resulting loss in revenues.

Even during war-to-peace transitions, when increases in government revenues are especially urgent, the IFIs have pressed for tariff reductions. At an October 1998 CG meeting on Guatemala, the IMF predicted that tax collections would fail to reach the target established in the peace accords; nevertheless, the IMF representative urged the Guatemalan authorities to 'resist pressures to increase import duties or delay the scheduled reduction in customs tariffs', warning that 'these actions will have adverse effects on output growth'.[32] Yet if revenue shortfalls lead to the unraveling of the peace process, the effects on output growth could be far more adverse.

In Rwanda, where the ratio of government revenue to national income is barely 10%, the IMF similarly has urged the government to reduce trade taxes. The Rwandan government cites 'a significant tariff reduction' as a reason for revenue shortfalls in its November 1999 Letter of Intent to the IMF, but then goes on to promise further reductions via the elimination of temporary import surcharges and all intra-regional tariffs.[33] Even in the wake of genocide, the fund's free-trade orthodoxy evidently trumped the fiscal needs of reconstruction.

Again, policymakers face a trade-off in choosing between the putative benefits of freer trade on the one hand, and the need for tariff revenues to help finance reconstruction on the other. Up to a point, higher tariffs will ease constraints on growth, rather than choke it off, by providing the government with resources to invest in peace. Beyond some point, excessively high tariffs could have adverse effects on economic performance. The challenge is to strike a reasonable balance between the short-term need for revenue and the long-term costs of trade protection. In war-torn societies there are often compelling reasons to put greater weight on the former.

Priorities for public spending

Peace accords create new priorities for public expenditure. Items at the top of the list typically include the creation of new democratic institutions, demobilisation of ex-combatants, protection of public security, and increased spending for health, education, and poverty reduction. Besides raising revenues, as discussed above, the other way governments can mobilise domestic resources for these purposes is to shift public spending from other activities.

After a civil war, some expenditure items can be regarded as 'negative priorities', in that they are inimical to the consolidation of peace. Military spending is a case in point. By reallocating resources from the armed forces to high-priority civilian needs, governments can not only reap a 'peace dividend' but also reduce their propensity to return to war. It is important to recognise, however, that certain categories of defence spending are crucial for building peace – including demobilisation programmes for soldiers, landmine clearance and the establishment of public security forces under civilian control. Apart from the level of military spending, therefore, key issues include its composition and transparency.

As illustrated in El Salvador, governments are sometimes reluctant to shift expenditure from the military to the high-priority programmes to which they agreed at the negotiating table. At the same time, the aid donors most able to influence domestic spending priorities – the IFIs – are sometimes reluctant to broach this 'political' issue. Yet as we have seen, economic considerations cannot be divorced from political ones in war-torn societies. The allocation of public expenditure has enormous consequences for the prospects of economic recovery as well as peace. Peace conditionality can encourage reorientation of domestic spending from wartime priorities to the new priorities of peacebuilding.

Aiming for equitable fiscal policies

Finally, fiscal policies can promote peace by aiming for a fair sharing of both the burdens of taxation and the benefits of public spending. Pro-peace policies can reduce disparities across ethnic, religious, regional and class divides, but inappropriate policies can exacerbate them. Given that state power often is in the hands of economically advantaged groups who are reluctant to tax themselves for the benefit of others, donor conditionality can serve as a useful countervailing force alongside the political mobilisation of those who stand to gain from more equitable fiscal policies.

On the revenue side, governments in countries emerging from civil war must not only increase taxes in order to finance investments in peace, but also do so in a fashion that eases rather than widens social cleavages. As discussed above in the case of Guatemala, luxury taxes on goods and services consumed primarily by the wealthiest strata of society can advance both aims, combining the administrative advantages of indirect taxation with strongly progressive distributional effects. Since many luxury goods are imported, they can be conveniently taxed at the point of entry via luxury tariffs.

In addition to advocating distributionally sensitive tax policies, aid donors could provide a positive 'demonstration effect' by ensuring that their own employees pay their fair share of local taxes. In the aftermath of a civil war, expatriate officials often count among a country's highest-paid residents and the main consumers of imported luxuries, from motor vehicles and air-conditioners to whisky and Coca-Cola. Yet these same individuals often are exempt from income taxes and customs duties, sending the message that rich and powerful people needn't pay taxes. Naturally, donor officials will not want to turn over a portion of their earnings to the government unless they believe that the proceeds will be used responsibly, and not squandered or diverted into private pockets. Paying local taxes would thus strengthen their incentive to insist on high standards of transparency and accountability in public expenditure.

On the spending side, too, governments face a dual challenge: to fund high-priority peace programmes, as discussed above, and also to ease social and economic disparities that can fuel violent conflict. This requires not simply more spending on sectors such as health and education, but also careful attention to the distribution of expenditure within these sectors, and reallocations in favour of disadvantaged groups. Public spending on primary healthcare and primary education, for example, has very different distributional effects from spending on hospital services or higher education.[34] Policies that foster an equitable distribution of the gains from government expenditure can also enhance public support for measures to increase tax revenues: citizens are more willing to pay taxes when they can see the benefits. The democratisation that often plays a central role in peace accords reinforces this political linkage between the revenue and expenditure sides of fiscal policy.

In summary, in countries emerging from civil war, aid donors need to rethink conditionality with respect to fiscal policy. There may be compelling reasons to relax orthodox deficit-reduction targets, while recognising that the adverse economic and political fallout from excessive deficits and hyperinflation limits the scope for relaxation. At the same time, donors need to pay far more attention to other key aspects of fiscal policy: the overall level of revenue and expenditure; priorities for public spending; and the distributional effects of both taxation and expenditure. Pro-peace fiscal policies do not require either looser or tighter conditions across-the-board, but rather a different mix of conditions tailored to the distinctive needs of the transition from war to peace.

Chapter 4

The Humanitarian Dilemma

In November 1998, shortly before the restoration of coalition rule in Cambodia, King Sihanouk met with a group of donor-country ambassadors in Phnom Penh. After thanking those donors who had continued to provide aid after the violent collapse of Cambodia's previous coalition government in July 1997, he urged the diplomats not to withhold aid so as to press the Hun Sen government to reach a new accommodation with its erstwhile partners. 'Aid sanctions will not hurt the leaders,' Sihanouk warned. 'They will only hurt the people. When the leaders need medical treatment, they go outside the country for it. When the leaders travel, they fly – they don't need the roads.'[1]

Sihanouk's plea underscored a basic dilemma in peace conditionality: vulnerability is inversely related to power. Withholding aid risks harming the poor, while leaving political leaders relatively unscathed. Yet unconditional aid can harm the poor, too, if it bolsters predatory leaders and jeopardises efforts to build a lasting peace. It is crucial to recognise that conditionality is not an all-or-nothing choice: it can be applied selectively to some types of aid but not to others. As a general rule, it makes sense to apply peace conditionality to the types of aid that are most valued by a country's political leaders and least valuable to its poorest and most vulnerable people.

This chapter examines some of the challenges of putting this principle into practice. The first section explores how even purely humanitarian aid can harm its intended beneficiaries by helping to fuel violent conflict. Yet withholding such aid can amount to 'punishing the poor'.[2] The next two sections consider policy responses to this dilemma: 'smart aid' and humanitarian exemptions from conditionality.

The spectre of the well-fed dead

Humanitarian agencies seek to mitigate the costs of war both by assisting civilians in need and by protecting them from violence. The first task often proves easier than the second. 'When we have access, seldom do we have the means of providing these groups with something that is more important than assistance, which is protection,' remarks UN Under Secretary-General Sergio Vieira de Mello. 'The spectre of the well-fed dead – those we feed but are unable to protect and eventually are killed – is something that we have been grappling with for many years now.'[3]

In recent years, critics have begun to explore the 'dark side' of humanitarian aid during civil conflicts – the ways in which aid itself can undermine the goal of protection. Four types of negative effects can be distinguished. First, humanitarian aid can be 'taxed' by the warring parties to help finance the conflict. Second, even if aid does not fund the conflict directly, it can do so indirectly by freeing domestic resources for war-making. Third, relief operations can serve as a smokescreen for inaction on other fronts by the donor governments. Finally, relief can also instill a false sense of security among the victims of the conflict, with potentially fatal results. The next few paragraphs expand briefly on these risks.

Political taxation of aid

During a war, it is not uncommon for some of the food, medicines, and other relief supplies intended for uprooted populations to be diverted into the hands of combatants. Such 'political taxation' can happen via the outright theft of relief shipments, or more subtly via the imposition of de facto levies on the non-combatants who receive aid.[4] This risk was illustrated in the 1980s in Cambodian refugee camps on the Thai border that were controlled by the Khmer Rouge. By day, international agencies delivered food and medicine to the camps. By night, Khmer Rouge fighters returned 'to rest, eat the food and use the medical supplies the agencies had provided, sleep with their wives, visit with their children, and recruit well-fed young refugees' – an arrangement that some observers termed an 'unholy alliance'.[5]

The plight of Rwandan refugees in eastern Zaire in 1994 again raised this same issue. Not only did the refugee camps include militiamen who had perpetrated genocide before being driven from Rwanda; militia leaders actually controlled the camps, using them as a base from which to regroup and rearm. 'It was the militiamen who determined food distribution and access to hospitals,' explained the head of one relief agency that chose to pull out of the camps. 'The refugees were more like hostages.'[6] By early 1996, the militia had launched attacks inside Rwanda, and soon the conflict spilled well beyond the country's borders.

Fungibility of aid

Even if humanitarian aid reaches civilians with minimal 'leakage' to combatants, it can fund conflict indirectly by reducing the need for the warring parties to devote their own resources to civilian welfare in territories under their control. The amount that the combatants' leadership would otherwise allocate to civilian purposes can seldom be calculated with much certainty, but the direction of this fungibility effect is clear: aid eases the trade-off between guns and butter (or guns and gruel), making possible a higher level of military spending for any given level of civilian welfare.

Relief as a substitute for action

A further criticism levelled at humanitarian relief does not concern the aid itself, but rather the inaction on other fronts that can accompany it. During the war in Bosnia, for example, humanitarian aid provided a veneer of international engagement at a time when Western governments were unwilling to act decisively to halt the conflict. Rather than complementing other forms of intervention, relief served as a substitute for them. Critics contend that humanitarian aid thereby became a mechanism by which ethnic cleansing was accommodated instead of confronted, a 'moral alibi to abstain from serious political engagement'.[7]

Illusions of safety

If humanitarian aid is similarly mistaken by its recipients as a token of deeper commitments by the international community, the results can be tragic. Rony Brauman, former president of Médicins Sans Frontières, suggests that aid to refugees in Srebrenica in the months before the town fell to the Bosnian–Serb forces 'helped maintain the illusion of international protection and thus encouraged the refugees to remain in the enclave rather than to seek a safer refuge'.[8] More blatantly, in eastern Zaire relief supplies were used to lure starving refugees into ambushes where they were massacred by Rwandan forces or their Congolese allies.[9]

In response to theses criticisms, defenders of humanitarian relief offer two compelling arguments. First, withholding aid would harm vulnerable non-combatants. In eastern Zaire, for example, most of the Rwandan refugees in the camps controlled by the *genocidaires* were innocent people, including roughly 750,000 children under the age of five.[10] Second, withholding aid may strengthen the hardline leaders it is meant to punish, by allowing them to monopolise the trade in basic necessities, closing off channels for interactions with the outside world, and letting them portray the denial of aid as further evidence of external hostility.

The humanitarian dilemma is summed up in the refugee's haunting question: 'You save my life today, but for what tomorrow?'[11] Providing aid can relieve immediate suffering, but at the risk of prolonging violence; withholding aid eventually may dampen violence, but at the risk of losing lives to hunger and disease. Donors confront a similar dilemma when providing 'postwar' reconstruction aid after civil wars. They must weigh the short-term benefits of providing aid, including the relief of human suffering, against the long-term costs of doing so in ways that could heighten the risk of renewed violence.

Smart aid

Donors do not face an either/or choice, however, of whether or not to provide aid. They also must choose how much to provide, of what types, to whom, and with what conditions attached. Conditionality does not require a threat to cut off all aid. Rather it can be applied selectively to the subset of aid that is of greatest benefit to political leaders and least benefit to at-risk populations. This policy can be termed 'smart aid'. It is akin to 'smart sanctions' that target the international economic interests of elite leaders, for example, by freezing their foreign bank accounts and restricting their freedom to travel, rather than targeting the population at large. In both cases, the aim is 'greater political gain and less civilian pain'.[12]

Faced with trade-offs between the positive and negative consequences of aid, a sensible decision-making rule is to weigh the good against the harm and then choose the best (or least bad) option. In assessing humanitarian impact, the most important consequences cannot be expressed simply in terms of money, as in conventional cost–benefit analysis of development projects. Instead the litmus test becomes numbers of lives protected and lost.

Yet the objective of protecting human lives may diverge from other important ends, such as human rights, justice and freedom. To take one example, efforts to pursue and punish war criminals may put lives at risk. One way to skirt such dilemmas is to elevate a single objective – such as the quest for justice, or the humanitarian imperative – above all else. But even those who embrace differing priorities generally acknowledge some need for trade-offs. If the only lives to be saved by humanitarian aid were those of war criminals who would thereby survive to perpetrate more violence, even the most ardent champion of the humanitarian imperative might have second thoughts. And few critics of humanitarian aid would advocate letting thousands of innocent people starve merely to deny succour to one or two war criminals in their midst. More than they sometimes admit, the participants in the humanitarian debate differ not so much on what values should count, but on how much they should count.

Although smart aid is attractive in principle, applying it in practice forces donors to confront deep ethical questions about the ends their aid is meant to serve. Moreover, regardless of how these questions are resolved, it would be imprudent to assume that donors will make consistently smart decisions. Like most decision-makers, they operate with incomplete information as well as imperfect foresight. The effects of conditionality will depend, for example, on the political and economic calculations of recalcitrant leaders, and on the extent to which the international community exerts diplomatic, trade, or military pressures on behalf of the same objectives. Furthermore, donor decisions may be deflected by other foreign-policy objectives and by the institutional cultures of aid agencies, as discussed in the next chapter. Given the difficulty of the moral dilemmas and the fallibility of the donors – and recognising that the costs of poor decisions include the suffering of innocent people – the smart aid principle should be implemented with caution.

Humanitarian exemptions

For these reasons, a good case can be made for a 'second-best' approach in which humanitarian aid is simply exempted from conditionality altogether. This approach would apply the 'smart aid' strategy, with its careful weighing of benefits and costs, only to non-humanitarian reconstruction and development aid. Humanitarian aid would not be subject to this test. This too poses a thorny problem: how to draw a clear line between humanitarian and non-humanitarian aid.

Donors have grappled with this classification problem in Bosnia. In 1997, after the Peace Implementation Council steering board declared that 'international economic aid is conditional upon compliance with, and implementation of, the Peace Agreement', an inter-agency Economic Task Force (ETF) chaired by the High Representative was established to develop guidelines for the application of peace conditionality.[13] In drafting guidelines for this purpose, the ETF adopted a selective approach that included exemptions for 'projects of a humanitarian nature, for example, food, basic medical care, sanitation and a minimum supply of power' (see Box 1).

Yet commodities such as food and medicine are not intrinsically 'humanitarian'; classification depends on the uses to which these goods are put. Food aid might not qualify as humanitarian assistance if it goes to feed soldiers. By the same token, the reconstruction of power plants might qualify as humanitarian assistance if the electricity goes to hospitals, but not if it goes to factories or to government offices.

Faced with the pitfalls of a commodity-based definition, donors sometimes opt instead for an agency-based definition, in

Box 1   Selective Conditionality in Bosnia

Excerpts from the Economic Task Force's 'Draft Guideline on the Application of Political Conditionality in Reconstruction Aid', August 1997

Donors and members of the Peace Implementation Council have taken the position that political conditionality should be applied in the implementation of the reconstruction aid programme. The objective is to give a new impetus to the peace process by rewarding those who cooperate and depriving from reconstruction aid those who obstruct the application of the Dayton Agreement ... .

The purpose of the present note is to set the basic rules which, according to the ETF [Economic Task Force], should govern the application of political conditionality ... .

1. *There will be no political conditionality for projects which are of humanitarian nature, e.g., food, basic medical care, sanitation and a minimum supply of power.*

2. *The following types of projects are to be privileged:*

   a) *projects promoting common and joint institutions and cooperation between the institutions of both entities ... ;*

   b) *projects fostering free movement within the country, e.g., basic repairs of roads and bridges;*

   c) *projects improving communication between people, e.g., media (if not government-controlled) and telecommunications;*

   d) *projects favoring the voluntary return of refugees ... .*

3. *For the projects mentioned in paragraph 2 above, political conditionality will be limited to excluding as beneficiaries:*

   a) *municipalities which actively obstruct the peace process, unless projects are specifically designed to foster cooperation in peace implementation;*

   b) *institutions (as project intermediaries) and companies (as contractors or credit takers) controlled by indicted war criminals or persons actively involved in obstructing the peace process.*

Continued

> 4. *For other projects (i.e., non-humanitarian and non-privileged projects), the political conditionality described in paragraph 3 will apply. In addition, donors are advised to:*
>
> a) *limit housing reconstruction to municipalities in priority return areas as designated by the RRTF [Reconstruction and Return Task Force], and/or participating in the Open Cities programme, and/or allowing significant minority returns; and*
> b) *consult with the ETF on the appropriate timing of projects exceeding US $10 million in aid prior to project approval or suspension on non-economic grounds.*

which aid delivered by humanitarian agencies is, by definition, 'humanitarian aid'. For example, aid through the European Community Humanitarian Office is classified as humanitarian, while other EU aid is not. While this definition has the merit of administrative convenience, it too provides a rather crude proxy for the distinction between humanitarian and non-humanitarian aid.

In principle, a better basis for defining humanitarian aid would be in terms of its effects: does the aid relieve human suffering by meeting basic human needs? By this definition, food aid counts as humanitarian if, and only if, it feeds people who otherwise are at risk of starvation. Even then, difficult questions persist. What if the food reaches hungry civilians, but also well-fed civilians, or hungry combatants? If its coverage is mixed – so that some of the aid serves basic human needs and some does not – does the ratio between them matter? Must the humanitarian share be at least 50:50, for example, to qualify for the exemption? Moreover, what if the delivery of humanitarian aid is politically manipulated for ends that are inimical to the consolidation of a lasting peace? In Bosnia, for example, some relief aid has been channelled through local Red Cross branches controlled by hard-line Bosnian–Croat nationalists. These local officials have withheld this aid from non-Croat 'minorities' (some of whom were demographic majorities in these localities before the war) who have attempted to return to their former homes. These same officials have used relief supplies to discourage displaced Croats now living in these communities from returning to their former homes elsewhere in Bosnia. Such families have been told that they will receive aid only if they register to vote in their new place of residence; if instead they exercise their right under the Dayton agreement to register in their former communities – thereby sig-nalling an intention to return – they too are denied relief.[14] These questions bring us inexorably back to the weighing of good and harm, the very task the humanitarian exemption is meant to circumvent.

When defined in terms of commodities or agencies, humani-tarian aid may appear to have little in common with reconstruction and development loans from the IFIs. When defined in terms of effects, however, the line between humanitarian and non-humanitarian aid can cross into this terrain. In 1997, for example the World Bank's resident representative in Sarajevo defended the Bank's intention to extend aid to Bosnia's Serb Republic on the grounds that 'much of our program is oriented towards humani-tarian-style investments'.[15] This eagerness to fund projects in the Serb Republic may have had less to do with humanitarian zeal than with the World Bank's need to win assent from the Serb member of Bosnia's collective presidency for loan agreements. But his remark left reporters to wonder what aid would not fit through a humanitarian loophole cut so generously as to include World Bank loans.

In 1998, the notion of extending humanitarian exemptions to the IFIs received an official imprimatur, when the Group of Eight (G-8) industrialised nations agreed to block some but not all IFI loans to India and Pakistan in the wake of their nuclear weapons tests. 'We do not wish to punish the peoples of India or Pakistan as a result of actions by their governments,' the G-8's communiqué stated, 'and we will therefore not oppose loans by the IFIs to meet basic human needs.'[16] The US Nuclear Nonproliferation Act of 1994 contains a similar clause, which like the G-8 statement does not define 'basic human needs', leaving considerable room for administrative discretion. In the case of India and Pakistan, the Clinton administration ultimately settled on a definition broad enough to exempt most World Bank loans from conditionality, in part because other G-8 countries favoured a softer stance, and in part because US businesses feared the loss of contracts and markets.

As these examples demonstrate, the delineation of 'humanitarian aid' that ought to be exempted from peace conditionality is not a straightforward matter. Apart from the conceptual difficulties of classifying aid in terms of commodities, agencies, or effects, political and institutional interests are likely to influence how commitments to humanitarian aims and building peace are translated into practice, an issue examined in the next chapter. In deciding whether or not to apply peace conditionality, and if so, to what types of aid, donors make choices that can mean the difference between life and death. But the fact that decisions are difficult does not mean that they can be avoided.

Chapter 5

Obstacles to Peace Conditionality

Efforts to use conditionality as a tool for building peace after civil wars must overcome three obstacles. First, peace is not the sole objective of donor governments, nor is it always the dominant one in shaping their interventions in war-torn societies. Competing objectives can militate against the use of peace conditionality. Second, aid agencies have their own organisational dynamics shaped by their incentive structures, ideological biases, and inter-agency rivalries. These can undermine agency effectiveness even in pursuit of more familiar development objectives, let alone in responding to the novel challenges of building peace. Third, the aid recipients that peace conditionality is meant to influence may object to it in the name of 'national sovereignty'. While these obstacles are formidable, none of them is insuperable. This chapter considers each in turn.

Competing 'national interests'

In addition to peace, donor governments often pursue other objectives in war-torn societies. These include geopolitical aims, economic and commercial interests, and the repatriation of refugees. Peace may advance these other objectives in the long run, but in the short run the pursuit of competing aims may skew donor policies away from those needed to consolidate a viable peace. Governments are also responsive to public opinion, however, and this can influence donor priorities in either direction.

Geopolitical aims

Far from promoting the peaceful resolution of social tensions, the Cold War rivalry between the industrial democracies and the Soviet bloc helped to fuel violent conflicts across Asia, Africa and Latin America. Official aid donors on both sides readily embraced conditionality – not for peace, but for Cold War aims. Aid was one weapon in the global contest. For example, because Cambodia's government in the 1980s was backed by the Soviet Union and Vietnam, the US not only withheld aid and diplomatic recognition, but went so far as to insist that the country's UN seat should remain in the hands of the murderous Khmer Rouge. As UN Secretary-General Kofi Annan recalls: 'Corruption and waste – indeed, results of any kind – were secondary to what donor countries wanted most, namely political allegiance.'[1]

Although the end of the Cold War eliminated this potent competing objective in foreign aid, geopolitical considerations can still impede the exercise of peace conditionality. For example, the French government's unwillingness to exercise peace conditionality in Rwanda in the crucial months between the August 1993 Arusha Peace Accord and the April 1994 genocide appears to have been driven, in no small measure, by the aim of backing the 'Francophone' Hutu against the 'Anglophone' Tutsi.[2] Even sympathetic observers of French policy lament this 'admittedly real, and altogether pathetic' linguistic rivalry.[3]

Such biases do not only affect bilateral aid. The policies of the IFIs, for example, are greatly influenced by the desires of the most powerful donor governments, who wield a preponderant share of voting power on the IFI boards. A recent World Bank study concedes that 'between 1970 and 1993 aid allocations – by bilateral and multilateral donors – were dominated by politics – both the international politics of the Cold War and the internal politics of aid agencies'.[4] The study cites aid to Mobutu's Zaire as 'just one of several examples where a steady flow of aid ignored, if not encouraged, incompetence, corruption, and misguided policies'.[5] The World Bank itself was among the biggest lenders to the Mobutu regime, accounting for $1.4bn of Zaire's $12.3bn external debt in 1994.[6] In the late 1980s, the pressure from powerful governments to lend to corrupt allies was so intense that a senior

IMF official warned that the fund's assistance was in danger of becoming 'indistinguishable from political support'.[7]

Economic and commercial interests

Economic interests routinely influence foreign policy. For example, securing access to key raw materials, such as oil, has long been seen as a major concern of the industrialised countries. More surprising, perhaps, is the extent to which more mundane commercial motives – for instance, the pursuit of contracts for building bridges or leasing aircraft – can drive donor decisions. Roughly half of all bilateral aid is 'tied' to imports of goods and services from the donor country.[8] In effect, tied aid is a vehicle by which donors subsidise overseas sales by their domestic private-sector constituents. Defenders of this practice argue that it builds 'essential political support' for foreign aid back home.[9] At the same time, aid becomes a means to win foreign political support for business constituents in the donor country.

This quest for short-term commercial advantage can erode the willingness of donors to exercise peace conditionality. In the mid-1990s, for example, the Cambodian government retaliated against the Australian government's criticism of its human rights record by cancelling business deals with several Australian companies. The lesson was not lost on other donors. 'What is important for many of these ambassadors is to defend their few miserable contracts,' a UN official in Phnom Penh observed. 'It is as if they represent their companies rather than their countries.'[10]

Recipient governments usually play quietly on these fears, but occasionally they do so openly. 'Japan is taking a lead,' a Cambodian commerce ministry official declared in 1999 while denouncing political conditions on US aid. 'By the time the US shapes up, if a US company is bidding on a contract against a Japanese company, do you think the US will win? I don't think so.'[11]

Refugee repatriation

In some cases, the desire to repatriate refugees is another important objective of aid donors – particularly when refugees are living in the donor countries. For example, some 345,000 Bosnians had taken refuge in Germany by the time of the Dayton Peace Agreement, and their support was costing German state and local governments approximately DM1,000 per refugee per month, or DM4bn (more than $2bn) per year.[12]

To expedite refugee returns to Bosnia, the German authorities deployed incentive packages, repatriation assistance, and threats of deportation. There is a tension, however, between this objective and the aim of consolidating a lasting peace. The quickest way to repatriate refugees is not to return them to their former homes, where those who expelled them often continue to wield power, but instead to send them to territories controlled by their 'own' people. So war-damaged houses rebuilt with donor aid are often occupied not by their original owners, but by returnees of the 'right' ethnicity – a practice that, in effect, converts refugees into internally displaced persons. This not only fails to advance the Dayton principle of ethnic reintegration, it also makes this goal still more difficult to achieve, since the return of the original owners to their homes now would require relocating the new occupants. Instead of using aid to encourage local authorities to accept minority returns, as discussed in Chapter 1, repatriation-driven reconstruction aid can help consolidate the demographic results of ethnic cleansing.

Public opinion

The conceptions of the 'national interest' that shape donor government policies respond, in part, to public opinion within donor countries. In some cases, this too operates against the use of peace conditionality. The US, for example, has been reluctant to exercise conditionality in its dealings with Israel – the top recipient of US foreign aid – in order to encourage progress toward a peace settlement with the Palestinians. 'If in the end Israel cannot accept our ideas, we will respect that decision,' US Ambassador Edward Walker assured leaders of the American Israel Public Affairs Committee (AIPAC) in 1998, 'and it will not affect our fundamental commitment to Israel by a single jot or tittle.'[13] This unconditional policy is often ascribed to the power of the pro-Israel lobby in the US, and AIPAC in particular, which *Fortune* magazine rates as the second most influential lobbying group in Washington.[14] But the deep-rooted antipathy towards the Palestinian side among some US politicians has acquired a momentum of its own. This was demonstrated in the mid-1990s, when in keeping with the official Israeli policy at that time, AIPAC arranged for senior international officials to brief key US Congressmen to urge them to fund the newly created Palestinian Authority. Despite AIPAC's lobbying efforts, Congress refused. 'We're not paying those terrorists!' an influential Congressman exclaimed to his visitors.[15]

Yet an informed and mobilised public opinion can also be a potent force for peace. When his aides brought him news of the Srebrenica massacre in July 1995, US President Bill Clinton reportedly exploded, 'I'm getting creamed!' A few days later, he complained to his foreign-policy advisers that the war in Bosnia was 'killing the US position of strength in the world'.[16] Ending the war had become identified with the president's own stature and with the US national interest. This same example shows that it would be a mistake, however, to overstate the impact of the so-called 'CNN effect'. For three years prior to the horror in Srebrenica, the international news media carried vivid news reports of the carnage in the former Yugoslavia, yet this failed to prompt decisive action by the Western powers. It is not raw images that drive policy, Michael Ignatieff observes, but the 'stories we tell' about these images.[17] Western political will to intervene in Bosnia emerged only when the war came to be seen not just as a story of human suffering, but as one of failed American and European leadership.

Nevertheless, the Bosnian case showed that when public opinion is sufficiently mobilised – and political leaders sufficiently accountable – it could lift peace to the top of the policy agenda. In the wake of a negotiated ending to a civil war, this can translate into backing for peace conditionality, helping to overcome the obstacles posed by competing geopolitical and economic objectives. In effect, public opinion can make a 'necessity of virtue'.[18] Yet even if governments conclude that peace is their overriding policy objective in aid to war-torn societies, the internal dynamics of the aid agencies can pose additional impediments to peace conditionality. The next section examines these obstacles.

Reforming donor agencies

Peace conditionality requires aid agencies to move beyond business as usual in several ways. First, they must reorient their
internal incentive structures to reward performance not in terms of
the quantity of aid disbursed, but rather in terms of the effects of
aid on the objective of building peace. Second, they must overcome
ideological biases that singlemindedly favour efficiency over equity
and the free market over state interventions. Third, they must work
to achieve greater coordination with other donors, tempering their
zeal to protect their own autonomy. Finally, they must become
more transparent and accountable to the public. The following
paragraphs outline the case for these reforms.

Changing incentive structures

Aid donors often measure success in terms of the amount of money
they disburse. More aid is axiomatically better than less. In the
early decades of foreign aid, inadequate investment in physical and
human capital was widely seen as the main barrier to economic
development. 'If money was the problem,' a recent World Bank
study observes, 'then "moving the money" was an appropriate
objective for aid and aid agencies.'[19] This translated into internal
incentive structures that emphasised the quantity of aid disbursed
over the quality of results achieved. Despite much discussion on
the need for outcome-based performance measures, the baneful
effects of the 'approval and disbursement culture' persist. At the
World Bank, for example, a recent internal review concluded that
project managers continue to see the volume of loan commitments
as an end in itself and appear to be willing to permit 'substantial'
sacrifices in quality in return for modest increases in the quantity
of lending.[20]

The incentives facing individual staff members often reflect
those facing the agencies themselves. 'Both donor and recipient
have incentive systems that reward reaching a high volume of
resource transfer, measured in relation to a predefined ceiling,' a
study for the Swedish International Development Authority remarks. 'Non-disbursed amounts will be noted by executive boards
or parliamentary committees and may result in reduced allocations
for the next fiscal year.'[21]

When aid is provided in the form of loans, as opposed to grants, there is an extra incentive: new lending helps ensure that recipients continue to service past debts. In December 1995, for example, the IMF heralded a $45m loan to Bosnia – the first loan issued under the Fund's new emergency credit window for 'post-conflict' countries – as 'a new beginning'.[22] But the loan's purpose was simply to allow the new Bosnian government to repay a bridge loan from the Dutch government, which in turn had been used to repay Bosnia's assessed share of the former Yugoslavia's arrears to the IMF. Old Yugoslavian debt was thereby transformed into new Bosnian debt.

Conditionality does not fit happily into these incentive structures. If institutions face penalties for withholding aid, but not for disbursing it unwisely, they can be expected to put a premium on 'moving the money'. If individual staff members are rewarded only for saying 'yes' but not for sometimes saying 'no', they will act accordingly. Peace conditionality requires that the performance of individuals and agencies be judged not in terms of how much aid they disburse, but in terms of how effectively this aid supports the goal of building a viable peace.

Overcoming ideological biases

Ideological fashions within the aid agencies can pose an additional impediment to peace conditionality. In keeping with the precepts of neoclassical economics, for instance, donors frequently focus narrowly on the goal of economic 'efficiency', neglecting the distributional issues of who gets what. This approach is singularly ill-suited to war-torn societies, where the prospects for peace often hinge on fragile balances of power, as discussed in Chapter 2. In assessing development projects and economic policies, donors must ask not only whether total benefits will exceed total costs – the usual bottom line in terms of efficiency – but also how the distribution of these benefits and costs will affect vertical disparities of class and horizontal cleavages of ethnicity, religion, race and region. These distributional consequences may be hard to measure but this does not mean that they can be safely ignored.

The ideological antipathy in some donor agencies to state interventions in economic affairs can also prove to be counterproductive in the wake of a civil war. If, for example, donors insist on tariff reductions in pursuit of the holy grail of free trade, this may reduce government revenues that are urgently needed to finance the costs of peace, as discussed in Chapter 3. Moreover, in some cases tariffs can help ease social tensions by protecting the livelihoods of vulnerable domestic producers. In El Salvador, for example, producer prices for maize and beans, the mainstays of peasant farming, have been undercut by cheap imports. Nevertheless, the World Bank has lauded the government's steep reductions in agricultural tariffs, arguing that 'to reintroduce protection could set precedents that could be extremely difficult to reverse in the future'.[23] This doctrinaire stance not only ignores the possibility that tariffs can be a 'second-best' remedy for market imperfections (including foreign agricultural subsidies and overvalued exchange rates that artificially depress world market prices), but also ignores the importance of an economically viable small-farm sector for the sustainability of the country's peace process. Again, policies must be judged in light of their impact on economic and political reconstruction, not on the basis of an *a priori* ideological dogma.

Improving inter-donor coordination

Effective peace conditionality also requires donors to grow beyond business as usual by improving coordination among themselves. If one donor insists, for example, that local authorities take steps to encourage minority returns in order to receive housing reconstruction aid, while another offers similar aid with weaker conditions or none at all, the lowest common denominator will prevail.

Inter-donor coordination may be more feasible following a civil war: in addition to the potential rewards being higher, international engagement in the peace process often leads to the creation of some coordination mechanisms inside and outside the country. The most ambitious examples of in-country coordination have been the Office of the High Representative (OHR) in Bosnia, and the Joint Liaison Committee and Local Aid Coordination Committee in Palestine. These are complemented by external coordination via the Peace Implementation Council steering board in the case of Bosnia, and the Ad Hoc Liaison Committee (AHLC) in the case of Palestine. The establishment of these coordination mechanisms has been far from smooth, however, and their success in overcoming inter-donor rivalries has been a matter of degree.

Although the OHR's powers in Bosnia are about as close as the contemporary world comes to a colonial administration, its ability to impose consistent policies on the donors is quite limited. The Dayton Peace Agreement specifies that in dealing with aid agencies, the High Representative shall 'respect their autonomy within their spheres of operation, while as necessary giving general guidance to them about the impact of their activities on the implementation of the peace settlement.'[24] In other words, the OHR must rely on persuasion, not authority. 'Here in Sarajevo,' a senior international envoy comments wryly, 'everyone wants coordination, but no one wants to be coordinated.'[25]

The difficulty in creating the AHLC to oversee aid to the PA is another case in point. The major powers decided to establish the committee in October 1993, shortly after the Oslo Accord between Israel and the PLO. Intense rivalries immediately emerged over the make-up of the committee. Tensions over who would chair the AHLC became so acute that at one point the Israelis and Palestinians jointly offered to mediate between the US and the EU – a rather striking turn of events. The battle ended with a compromise in which Norway became chair.

In choosing the extent to which they will coordinate their programmes and policies, donors must weigh the benefits of greater coherence against the costs of reduced autonomy. Like most institutions, aid agencies tend to zealously guard their prerogatives. But the benefits to be gained from a consistent approach to peace conditionality greatly increase the potential reward from improved coordination. In some cases, this might even involve ceding a degree of control – over the setting and enforcement of conditions, if not over budgetary allocations – to an international body established for this purpose.

Increasing donor transparency and accountability

The reforms in donor agencies outlined above could be facilitated by moves toward greater transparency and accountability in decision-making. The credibility of donor calls for 'good governance' in aid-receiving countries will be strengthened if they practise what they preach. At the same time, stronger public oversight could encourage the agencies to elevate results above disbursements, question their ideological presuppositions, and better coordinate their activities to demonstrate success. World Bank president James Wolfensohn's recent call for the creation of 'independent verification and evaluation systems open to civil society' is an encouraging sign of movement in this direction.[26]

A plausible objection to peace conditionality is that we cannot be confident that the aid donors will 'get it right'. Indeed we may expect them frequently to 'get it wrong', whether due to simple ineptitude or the political, economic, and institutional biases outlined above. In foreign policy, Stanley Hoffmann has observed, the danger of ineffective idealism is compounded by the danger of 'effective hypocrisy'.[27] This risk cannot be dismissed lightly. Yet aid inevitably helps to shape the course of events in recipient countries for good or ill. Peace conditionality does not expand the power of donors or magnify their potential to do harm; rather, it orients this power more systematically to the goal of constructing and consolidating a durable peace. Increased transparency and accountability would not guarantee this reorientation, but they could help it along, while providing a democratic check on ineptitude and hypocrisy. However imperfect, the result is likely to be an improvement over the status quo.

Whose sovereignty?

A final obstacle to peace conditionality is the objection that it trespasses on national sovereignty. There are three responses to this concern. First, aid recipients are free to accept or reject the aid-for-peace bargain. Insofar as aid impinges on national sovereignty, this is due not to conditions tied to the aid but rather to the need for aid itself. Second, nations are not unitary actors. Policies that dilute the 'sovereignty' of some groups or individuals within a country may strengthen that of others. Finally, national sovereignty is not an ultimate end but rather a means toward the more fundamental aims of individual sovereignty and human well-being. The case for peace conditionality rests on its ability to advance these latter goals.

Donors are often said to 'impose' conditions on aid recipients, reflecting the fact that these stipulated conditions are often unwelcome to some people in the recipient country. Indeed, if the conditions met with universal favour, they would be superfluous. The view that donors 'impose' conditions rests implicitly on the counterfactual possibility of unconditional aid. Whatever its hypothetical appeal, however, this lacks any sound basis in international realities. International mechanisms for automatic aid flows do not exist, nor are they likely to be created anytime soon. In their absence, aid conditionality differs from trade sanctions, to which the verb 'impose' is more accurately applied. Trade sanctions block private transactions that would occur in the absence of government intervention, whereas aid itself is a government intervention.

To be sure, aid donors and recipients do not come to the bargaining table with equal power. The more desperately the recipient needs aid, the greater the leverage of the donor. In this sense, the very need for aid compromises the recipient's sovereignty. Moreover, as noted above, with conditions or without them, large injections of foreign aid into a nation's body politic invariably impinge on 'national sovereignty' in the broad sense of freedom from external influence. Aid changes the size and distribution of the economic pie, and with it the balances of power in the recipient country. The question is not whether aid will have such effects, but what they will be.

The term 'national' sovereignty conveys the deceptive idea that nations can be regarded as unitary actors. Yet every nation comprises groups and individuals with diverse – and often divergent – interests. Control of the state, the ostensible vessel of national sovereignty, changes hands over time and typically is contested at any point in time. The sharper the contests for state power, the less clear it is whose sovereignty is identified with the nation's. Nowhere are these contests sharper, and the identification of parties with the nation more problematic, than in countries torn by civil war.

There are multiple actors and interests on the donor side too, as we have seen. So beneath the aid-for-peace bargain between 'the' donor and 'the' recipient lies a more complex relationship: an alliance among internal and external actors who embrace peace-building as their overriding goal. Peace conditionality does not seek to impose outside ideas or values on the recipient country. Rather it brings the leverage of donors to bear on behalf of a reform agenda to which recipients have already committed themselves in the peace accords. Though this agenda has substantial domestic 'ownership', it remains subject to foot dragging, back-tracking, and outright opposition – hence the need for external allies.

In recent decades, national sovereignty increasingly has come to be seen not as an ultimate end but as a means to advance the more fundamental goal of human freedom or 'individual sovereignty'. UN Secretary-General Annan referred to this historic shift in a September 1999 address to the General Assembly:

> *State sovereignty, in its most basic sense, is being redefined by the forces of globalisation and international cooperation. The State is now widely understood to be the servant of its people, and not vice versa. At the same time, individual sovereignty – and by this I mean the human rights and fundamental freedoms of each and every individual as enshrined in our Charter – has been enhanced by a renewed consciousness of the right of every individual to control his or her own destiny.*[28]

National sovereignty need not conflict with individual sovereignty. When the state is indeed 'the servant of its people', the two complement each other. When they come into conflict, however – when states violate the human rights and fundamental freedoms of their citizens – then the international community must decide which takes precedence. Peace conditionality puts the sovereignty of individuals ahead of the preferences of politicians for aid without strings.

Efforts to apply peace conditionality must surmount all three sets of obstacles discussed in this chapter: the competing priorities of donor governments, the inertia of business as usual at the aid agencies, and objections raised in the name of national sovereignty. Overcoming these obstacles is not a small task, but neither is building peace.

Conclusion

The signing of a peace accord can mark a watershed in the transition from war to peace, or merely a brief respite from violent conflict. External aid cannot guarantee a lasting peace, but it can help to make this outcome more likely. How well aid serves this purpose depends not only on its quantity but also on its qualities: what types of aid are provided, to whom, and what conditions are attached.

Peace conditionality – formal performance criteria or informal policy dialogue that makes aid conditional on efforts by recipients to implement peace accords and consolidate the peace – can strengthen the incentives for ending conflict and discourage a return to war. In Chapter 1, we saw that the grand bargain embodied in the pledges of aid unlocked by the signing of a peace accord can be followed by mini-bargains, whereby specific types of aid are tied to specific steps to build peace. The priorities for such aid-for-peace bargains will vary from case to case. In some times and places, as in El Salvador and Guatemala, a key issue may be the need to mobilise domestic resources for peace programmes by increasing tax revenues and reorienting public spending. In others, as in Cambodia, the key issues may be protecting human rights and preventing the looting of the country's natural resources. In still others, as in Bosnia, central concerns may include ensuring that displaced people are free to return to their homes and that they secure equitable access to employment, schools, housing, and personal safety.

To be sure, peace conditionality on its own will seldom be enough to ensure a successful transition from war to peace. Apart from aid, the international community may need to use other tools, including diplomacy, trade, and the deployment of peacekeeping forces, to support this transition. To expect aid and conditionality to bear the entire burden would often be a recipe for failure. Moreover, some peace agreements are doomed to fail due to their own inherent flaws, regardless of international backing. But to recognise that peace conditionality is not sufficient to build a durable peace is not to say that it is not necessary.

If donors wish to invest wisely in peace, they must make difficult decisions: how to distribute aid in a fractured and fractious society? How to make sure that external resources 'crowd in' domestic resources – that is, encourage local investment in the movement toward peace – rather than crowd them out? How to combine immediate humanitarian relief with the long-term objective of ending violent conflict?

In the day-to-day business of supplying aid to developing countries, donors often avoid such 'political' questions. Rather than dealing with the sensitive issue of who gets what, they focus to creating a bigger economic pie, leaving it to the country's rulers to decide how it will be sliced. Rather than attempting to influence the size and composition of public revenue and expenditure, donors typically focus on the need to control the government's budget deficit. Rather than facing the ethical dilemmas that arise when humanitarian aid helps to prolong violent conflict, donors often adopt either/or stances: the relief agencies champion the humanitarian imperative to save lives in the short run, while the foreign ministries downplay humanitarian needs in favour of long-term strategic goals.

These evasions, questionable even in 'normal' times, are untenable in cases of aid to societies that have embarked on the uncertain road from war to peace. To shift all responsibility for the distributional consequences of aid to the recipient government is not a 'neutral' policy when the government represents one party to the conflict. To pretend that the sole litmus test of a sound fiscal policy is a small budget deficit is myopic when other pressing issues include how to ease social tensions and how to fund the costs of peace. To pursue short-term humanitarian aims or the long-term goal of building peace, while ignoring the potential trade-offs between the two, is to play fast and loose with the lives of other people.

In Chapter 2 we saw that the distributional impacts of aid are critical for the implementation of peace accords and the consolidation of peace. Aid can strengthen the hand of proponents of the negotiated settlement vis-à-vis hardline opponents within their own parties; at the same time, aid can help maintain the balance of power between the contending parties to the conflict, so that neither side becomes so powerful as to be able to resort to violence with impunity, nor so desperate as to do so as the only alternative to subjugation. If, instead, distribution-blind aid ends up in the hands of those opposed to peace or tilts the balance of power decisively to one side, it can jeopardise the peace process. Aid can help to consolidate peace by fostering inclusive economic growth and an inclusive political environment. The pursuit of these goals again requires careful attention to the impacts of aid on the distribution of wealth and power. In war-torn societies, aid must aim not only to expand the economic pie but also to redress the social disparities among classes, regions, or religious and ethnic groups that fuelled war. If, instead, distribution-blind aid perpetuates or exacerbates these disparities, it can set the stage for renewed violence. Conditionality related to distributional impacts can help make aid a more effective tool for building peace.

In Chapter 3 we saw that peace accords have significant implications for fiscal policy, an arena in which the IFIs play a key role. The IFIs' conventional preoccupation with the need to trim government budget deficits in the name of macroeconomic stability is ill-suited to societies embarked on war-to-peace transitions, where political stability is equally crucial for investment and economic performance. After a civil war, critical fiscal policy issues include the total magnitude of public revenue and expenditure, the share of government spending devoted to high-priority peace programmes, and the distributional incidence of taxation and expenditure. In some cases, there may be trade-offs among these fiscal objectives. For example, the urgent need to fund high-priority peace programmes may require a larger budget deficit, or the need to ensure that taxation has progressive distributional impacts may rule out some otherwise attractive ways of raising revenue. Such trade-offs are seldom best resolved by elevating a single yardstick of fiscal discipline above all others. Conditionality attuned to all these dimensions of fiscal policy can help make aid a more powerful lever for peace.

In Chapter 4 we saw that the humanitarian dilemma arises in war-torn societies regardless of whether or not aid donors choose to exercise peace conditionality. To withhold aid so as to leverage compliance with peace accords could harm people in need. But unconditional aid that brings short-term relief at the expense of long-term efforts to establish peace raises the spectre of the 'well-fed dead'. Again, the best way to address this dilemma is not to ignore it by elevating the short term over the long term, or vice versa, but rather to seek to ease the trade-offs, applying conditions selectively to some types of aid and not others. 'Smart aid' would apply conditionality first and foremost to the aid that is most valued by political leaders; humanitarian exemptions would protect the aid that is most vital to vulnerable populations.

Finally, in Chapter 5 we saw that the obstacles to successful aid-for-peace bargains do not lie only on the recipient side of the aid relationship. On the donor side, too, the willingness of governments to make peace their overriding priority is limited by competing foreign policy interests, and the ability of aid agencies to exercise peace conditionality is limited by their own institutional cultures. Concerns about 'national sovereignty' can present a further obstacle. Peace conditionality cannot simply be grafted on to the existing menu of policy options, leaving all else unchanged. It will require a reorientation of donor government priorities, so that building peace prevails over narrower political and economic concerns. It will require a restructuring of incentives within the aid agencies, to emphasise the quality of results achieved over the quantity of money disbursed. And it will require world public opinion and world leaders to continue the historic movement toward policies founded on respect for the sovereignty of individual human beings. The challenges of building peace thus extend beyond the reconstruction of war-torn societies to the reconstruction of aid itself.

Notes

Acknowledgements

I am grateful for the facilities made available to me at Oxford University by Queen Elizabeth House and its director, Professor Frances Stewart, where I began the research on which this essay is based. My research and writing were supported by grants from the John D. and Catherine T. MacArthur Foundation and the United States Institute of Peace.

My research depended on the generosity of the many individuals who agreed to share their knowledge and opinions in interviews. I owe special debts of gratitude to Sandy Coliver and Chris Bennett for their guidance in Bosnia; Jean Arnault, David Holiday, and Pablo Rodas for their assistance in Guatemala; Joel Charny and Christophe Peschoux for their insights in Cambodia; Rex Brynen, Charles Shammas, and Gidi Gerstein for introducing me to diverse perspectives in Palestine and Israel; and Anders Kompass, who first encouraged me to explore the interface between economic policy and peace-building in El Salvador. I have also benefited greatly from conversations over the years with Nicole Ball, Nat Colletta, Shep Forman, Steve Holtzman, Alcira Kreimer, Philippe LeBillon, Manuel Pastor, Stewart Patrick, Peter Uvin, Tony Vaux, George Vickers, Teresa Whitfield, and Elisabeth Wood.

Introduction

[1] Marc Kaufman, 'US Meeting Envisions Rebuilding Afghanistan,' *Washington Post*, 21 November 2001, p. A3.

[2] James K. Boyce *et al.*, *Adjustment Toward Peace: Economic Policy and Post-War Reconstruction in El Salvador*, report prepared for the United Nations Development Programme, San Salvador, May 1995. A revised version of this study was published as James K. Boyce, ed., *Economic Policy for Building Peace: The Lessons of El Salvador* (Boulder: Lynne Rienner, 1996) and in Spanish as *Ajuste Hacia la Paz: La política económica y la reconstrucción de posguerra en El Salvador* (Mexico City: Plaza y Valdes, 1999).

[3] The phrase is Michael E. Brown's; see his edited volume, *The International Dimensions of Internal Conflict* (Cambridge, MA: MIT Press, 1996), p. 625.

4 See, for example, Christopher L. Gilbert, Andrew Powell and David Vines, 'Positioning the World Bank,' and Paul Collier, 'Conditionality, dependence and coordination: three current debates in aid policy,' both in Christopher L. Gilbert and David Vines, eds, *The World Bank: Structures and Policies* (Cambridge: Cambridge University Press, 2000).

Chapter 1

1 Secretary of State Madeleine K. Albright, *Intervention at Peace Implementation Council Ministerial Meeting, Sintra, Portugal, 30 May 1997*, as released by the Office of the Spokesman in Sintra, Portugal, US Department of State.

2 See 'Council conclusions on guidelines for former Yugoslavia,' *Bulletin of the European Union*, 10–1995, pp. 138–41; Europe Information Service, Euro-East, 'EU/Former Yugoslavia: Talks Move to Brussels as Plans Coalesce,' 24 October 1995; and Guy Dinsmore, 'EU Says Political Conditions Attached to Bosnian Aid,' Reuters wirefeed, 26 January 1996.

3 European Commission and World Bank, 'Chairman's Conclusions of the Second Donors' Conference on the Reconstruction of Bosnia and Herzegovina,' Brussels, 13 April 1996. See also World Bank press release no. 96/S56, 'Donors pledge $1.23 Billion to Help Rebuild Bosnia: Total Available for 1996 Reconstruction now exceeds $1.8 billion.'

4 For an account, see Laura Silber and Allan Little, *The Death of Yugoslavia* (London: Penguin, 1996), pp. 291–302.

5 *Political Declaration from Ministerial Meeting of the Steering Board of the Peace Implementation Council,* Sintra, Portugal, 30 May 1997, paragraph 46.

6 UNHCR, *Open Cities Initiative* (Sarajevo: Office of the Special Envoy and Office of the Chief of Mission, 31 August 1997).

7 See Nicola Dahrendorf and Hrair Balian, 'Case Study: Bosnia and Herzegovina,' OECD Development Assistance Committee, Task Force on Conflict, Peace and Development, Workshop on the Limits and Scope for the Use of Development Co-operation Incentives and Disincentives for Influencing Conflict Situations, Paris, 3–4 May 1999, para. 104; and International Crisis Group, 'Bosnia's Refugee Logjam Breaks: Is the International Community Ready?', Sarajevo, 30 May 2000.

8 International Crisis Group, 'Bosnia: Minority Employment Principles: An ICG Proposal,' Sarajevo, 1 December 1998.

9 On the role of trade in sustaining violent conflict, see David Keen, *The Economic Functions of Violence in Civil Wars*, Adelphi Paper 320 (Oxford: Oxford University Press for the International Institute of Strategic Studies, 1998).

10 Stephen John Stedman, 'Spoiler Problems in Peace Processes,' *International Security*, vol. 22, no. 2, Fall 1997, pp. 5–53.

11 See Elizabeth S. Rogers, 'Economic Sanctions and Internal Conflict,' in Michael E. Brown, ed., *The International Dimensions of Internal Conflict* (Cambridge, MA: MIT Press, 1996), pp. 411–34.

12 For an account of the US moves, which also included suspension of bilateral aid and a threat to freeze IFI lending, see Rachel M. McCleary, *Dictating Democracy: Guatemala and the End of Violent Revolution* (Gainesville: University Press of Florida, 1999). McCleary argues that many in Guatemala's

private sector did not, in fact, need this extra encouragement to oppose the coup.

[13] David Cortright and George A. Lopez, *The Sanctions Decade: Assessing UN Strategies in the 1990s* (Boulder: Lynne Rienner, 2000).

[14] Michael W. Doyle, *UN Peacekeeping in Cambodia: UNTAC's Civil Mandate* (Boulder: Lynne Rienner, 1995), p. 87.

[15] See *A Rough Trade: The Role of Companies and Governments in the Angolan Conflict* (London: Global Witness, December 1998); and Lynne Duke, 'Angola Is Afloat in Oil, but Where's the Money?' *International Herald Tribune*, 4 January 1999, p. 7.

[16] United Nations Security Council, *Report of the Panel of Experts on Violations of Security Council Sanctions Against UNITA*, S/2000/203, 10 March 2000; IMF, *Angola: Memorandum of Economic and Financial Policies*, 3 April 2000. See also Rachel L. Swarns, 'In Oil Bonanza, Frail Visions of a New Angola,' *New York Times*, 24 September 2000, pp. A1, 8.

[17] World Bank, *The World Bank's Experience with Post-conflict Reconstruction. Volume V: Desk Reviews of Cambodia, Eritrea, Haiti, Lebanon, Rwanda, and Sri Lanka*, Report No. 17769, 4 May 1998, pp. 23, 30.

[18] See, for example, Pablo Mauro, 'Why Worry About Corruption?' Economic Issues series no. 6, IMF, February 1997; and 'Helping Countries Combat Corruption: The Role of the World Bank,' World Bank, Poverty Reduction and Economic Management Network, September 1997.

Chapter 2

[1] Charles King, *Ending Civil Wars*, Adelphi Paper 308 (Oxford: Oxford University Press for the International Institute of Strategic Studies, 1997), p. 40.

[2] Peter Uvin, *Aiding Violence: The Development Enterprise in Rwanda* (West Hartford: Kumarian Press, 1998), p. 237.

[3] International Bank for Reconstruction and Development, *Articles of Agreement*, Article III, Section 5(b).

[4] House of Commons, International Development Committee, *Conflict Prevention and Post-Conflict Reconstruction. Volume I: Report and Proceedings* (London: The Stationery Office, 1999), para. 59.

[5] William Shawcross, *Cambodia's New Deal* (Washington DC: Carnegie Endowment for International Peace, 1994), pp. 17, 47–48. For details, see the reports by the London-based NGO Global Witness, including 'Forests, Famine and War: The Key to Cambodia's Future' (March 1995) and 'Thai-Khmer Rouge Links & the Illegal Trade in Cambodia's Timber' (July 1995).

[6] Doyle, p. 29; E.V.K. FitzGerald, 'The Economic Dimension of Social Development and the Peace Process in Cambodia' in Peter Utting, ed., *Between Hope and Insecurity: The Social Consequences of the Cambodian Peace Process* (Geneva: UN Research Institute for Social Development, 1994), p. 81; Shawcross, p. 32.

[7] World Bank, *The World Bank's Experience with Post-conflict Reconstruction: Volume V: Desk Reviews of Cambodia, Eritrea, Haiti, Lebanon, Rwanda, and Sri Lanka*. Report No. 17769, 4 May 1998, p. 10.

[8] Grant Curtis, *Cambodia Reborn? The Transition to Development and Democracy* (Washington DC: Brookings Institution, 1998), p. 78.

[9] World Bank (1998), p. 8.

[10] *Ibid.*, p. 23; and Doyle, p. 51.

11 Shawcross, p. 28.
12 World Bank (1998), p. 5.
13 *Ibid.*, p. 25.
14 Personal interview, Washington DC, June 1997.
15 Statement by Hubert Neiss, IMF Representative, Consultative Group Meeting, Paris, 1–2 July 1997, p. 2. Mr. Neiss's remarks appear in the proceedings of the meeting, published by the Council for the Development of Cambodia.
16 Letter from Javad Khalilzadeh-Shirazi, Chairman, Cambodia Consultative Group Meeting, 1997, to HRH Prince Norodom Ranariddh, First Co-Prime Minister and H.E. Samdech Hun Sen, Second Co-Prime Minister, Paris, 2 July 1997.
17 Personal interview, Phnom Penh, November 1998.
18 Global Witness, a London-based NGO, played a leading role in exposing illegal logging and encouraging the aid donors to respond; for documentation, see http://www.oneworld.org/globalwitness. See also Philippe LeBillon, 'The Political Ecology of Transition in Cambodia 1989–1999: War, Peace and Forest Exploitation,' *Development and Change*, vol. 31, no. 4, September 2000.
19 Thomas Carothers, 'The Rule of Law Revival,' *Foreign Affairs*, vol. 77, no. 2, March/April 1998, p. 96.
20 *Bosnia and Hercegovina. The Unindicted: Reaping the Rewards of 'Ethnic Cleansing'* (New York and London: Human Rights Watch, January 1997). See also Diane Paul, 'Aiding and Abetting,' *War Report* (London: Institute for War and Peace Reporting, May 1997), No. 51, pp. 30–1.
21 Quoted in Kurt Schork, 'Donors Debate Fine-tuning Bosnian Aid,'

Reuters European Business Report, November 29, 1996.
22 'Summary Report: Donor Aid to BiH, December 1, 1999,' *OHR Economic Newsletter*, vol. 2, no. 11.
23 See Bonn Peace Implementation Conference, *Conclusions: Bosnia and Herzegovina 1998: Self-sustaining Structures*, 10 December 1997, section III.1.g.; and R. Jeffrey Smith, 'Legal Ethnic Cleansing Keeps Sarajevo Muslim,' *International Herald Tribune*, 3 February 1998, p. 4.
24 Personal interview, Washington DC, December 1997.
25 One such technique is to count equal percentage changes in income equally, no matter to whom they accrue. See James K. Boyce, 'Let Them Eat Risk: Wealth, Rights, and Disaster Vulnerability,' *Disasters*, vol. 24, no. 3, September 2000.
26 Similarly, 'ethno-national' impact assessments have been suggested by Wolfgang H. Reinicke, 'Can International Financial Institutions Prevent Internal Violence? The Sources of Ethno-National Conflict in Transitional Societies,' in A. & A.H. Chayes, eds, *Preventing Conflict in the Post-Communist World* (Washington DC: Brookings Institution, 1996). See also Kenneth Bush, *A Measure of Peace: Peace and Conflict Impact Assessment of Development Projects in Conflict Zones* (Ottawa: International Development Research Centre, March 1998).
27 The need for conflict impact assessments has now been recognised by the British and Canadian governments and by the EU. See House of Commons, International Development Committee, *Sixth Report: Conflict Prevention and Post-conflict Reconstruction*, Vol. 2, para. 34 (London: The Stationery Office, August 1999).

Chapter 3

1. Mirna Lievano de Marques, 'Statement on the Stabilization and Adjustment Program and National Reconstruction Program of El Salvador,' Annex III in World Bank, *Chairman's Report of Proceedings: Consultative Group for El Salvador, Washington DC, March 23, 1992* (author's translation from the Spanish).

2. World Bank, *Chairman's Report*, p. 5.

3. Quoted in James K. Boyce, 'External Resource Mobilization,' in James K. Boyce, ed., *Economic Policy for Building Peace: The Lessons of El Salvador*, Boulder: Lynne Rienner, 1996, p. 130.

4. 'Stabilization and Adjustment: Progress and Future Agenda,' Statement of the IBRD [World Bank] Representative at the Consultative Group Meeting for El Salvador, Paris, 1 April 1993, p. 6.

5. 'CG Meeting on El Salvador, 1 April 1993 – Nordic Statement,' pp. 3–4.

6. Boyce, p. 144. Excluding expenditure for the police, El Salvador's military spending in 1993 reportedly amounted to 1.5 percent of GDP (Graciana del Castillo, 'Post-Conflict Reconstruction and the Challenge to International Organizations: El Salvador: An Illustrative Case,' IMF Working Paper, January 1999, p. 47).

7. For details on these and other financing gaps, see Boyce, pp. 132–3.

8. Alvaro de Soto and Graciana del Castillo, 'Obstacles to Peacebuilding,' *Foreign Policy*, No. 94, Spring 1994, pp. 69–83.

9. Michael W. Foley with George R. Vickers and Geoff Thale, 'Land, Peace, and Participation: The Development of Post-War Agricultural Policy in El Salvador and the Role of the World Bank,' Washington DC: Washington Office on Latin America, Occasional Paper, 12 June 1997.

10. See Carlos Acevedo, 'Structural Adjustment, the Agricultural Sector, and the Peace Process,' in James K. Boyce, ed., *Economic Policy for Building Peace: The Lessons of El Salvador* (Boulder: Lynne Rienner, 1996), pp. 209–31.

11. Tommie Sue Montgomery, 'Constructing Democracy in El Salvador,' *Current History*, February 1997, pp. 61–7.

12. World Bank, *World Development Indicators 1998* (Washington DC: World Bank, 1998).

13. World Bank, *The World Bank's Experience with Post-conflict Reconstruction. Volume III: El Salvador Case Study*, 4 May 1998, p. 41.

14. *Ibid.*, p. 51.

15. Other major Guatemalan peace accords dealt with human rights (March 1994), the resettlement of uprooted populations (June 1994), the rights and identity of indigenous peoples (March 1995), and military and police restructuring (September 1996).

16. The continuities are personal as well as institutional: UN mediator Arnault subsequently became the head of MINUGUA, the UN mission in Guatemala charged with verification of implementation of the accords, and the World Bank staff member who assisted him in drafting the socio-economic accord became the bank's resident representative in Guatemala.

17. Personal interview, Washington DC, April 1999.

18. The 12% tax-ratio target represented a concession by the URNG, which initially proposed a 17% target, and then conceded to a target of 14%. In a rather unusual alliance, the URNG and

the IMF both pressed for the latter target, while the government's negotiators argued for a lower one (interviews with senior URNG and IMF officials, Guatemala City and Washington DC, December 1997).

[19] Milka Casanegra de Jantscher *et al.*, 'Guatemala: Rompiendo la Barrera del 8 Por Ciento,' Washington DC: IMF, Department of Public Finance, May 1997, p. 2.

[20] World Bank, *Memorandum of the President of the International Bank for Reconstruction and Development to the Executive Directors on a Country Assistance Strategy of the World Bank Group for the Republic of Guatemala*, draft, June 1998, p. 22.

[21] MINUGUA, 'El Pacto Fiscal: Un año después,' May 2001.

[22] Peace Secretariat, Government of the Republic of Guatemala, 'Advances in the Compliance of the Commitments Derived from the Peace Agreements,' 30 November 2001, para. 93.

[23] MINUGUA, 'El Pacto Fiscal …', p. 9.

[24] Daniel L. Wisecarver, 'Impuestos en Guatemala: Recaudacion suficiente con progresividad global.' Document prepared for the Preparatory Commission of the Pacto Fiscal, 20 September 1999, p. 54.

[25] Michael Best, 'Political Power and Tax Revenues in Central America,' *World Development*, Vol. 3, 1974, p. 52.

[26] Personal interview, Phnom Penh, November 1998.

[27] World Bank, *The World Bank's Experience with Post-conflict Reconstruction: Volume V: Desk Reviews of Cambodia, Eritrea, Haiti, Lebanon, Rwanda, and Sri Lanka.* Report No. 17769, 4 May 1998, pp. 15, 29, 34.

[28] 'Donor Statement' dated 6 October 1995, cited by Christian Michelsen Institute, *Evaluation of Norwegian Assistance to Peace, Reconciliation and Rehabilitation in Mozambique* (Oslo: Ministry of Foreign Affairs, 1997), p. 49. For discussion, see Joseph Hanlon, *Peace Without Profit* (Oxford: James Currey, 1996), pp. 134–8; and Nicole Ball and Sam Barnes, 'Mozambique,' in Shepard Forman and Stewart Patrick, eds, *Good Intentions: Pledges of Aid for Post-Conflict Recovery* (Boulder: Lynne Rienner, 2000), p. 195.

[29] For further discussion, see Manuel Pastor and James K. Boyce, 'El Salvador: Economic Disparities, External Intervention, and Civil Conflict,' in E. Wayne Nafziger, Frances Stewart, and Raimo Vayrynen, eds, *War, Hunger, and Displacement: The Origins of Humanitarian Emergencies. Volume 2: Case Studies* (Oxford: Oxford University Press, 2000), pp. 365–400.

[30] Tax revenues in El Salvador and Guatemala in 1996 were 11.6% and 7.7% of GDP, respectively (World Bank, *World Development Report 1998/99*, New York: Oxford University Press, 1998, p. 216). In Cambodia in 1995, the corresponding figure was 6.2% (IMF, *Cambodia – Recent Economic Developments*, IMF Staff Country Report 97/9, March 1997, p. 17). In Bosnia in 1997, it was 13.5% for the Federation; GDP data for Bosnia's Serb Republic were not available (calculated from data in Economic Task Force Secretariat, *Newsletter*, Sarajevo: Office of the High Representative, Vol. 1, Issues 1 and 2).

[31] Joseph E. Stiglitz, *Economics of the Public Sector*, 2nd edn (New York: W.W. Norton, 1988), p. 388.

[32] Statement by the IMF Staff Representative at the Consultative Group Meeting on Guatemala, Brussels, 22–23 October 1998.

[33] *Memorandum of Economic and Financial Policies of the Government of Rwanda for 1999/2000 (July–June)*, 2 November 1999, para. 5 and box 3 (http://www.imf.org/external/np/loi/1999/110299.HTM).

[34] Dominique van de Walle and Kimberly Nead, eds, *Public Spending and the Poor: Theory and Evidence* (Baltimore and London: Johns Hopkins University Press, 1995).

Chapter 4

[1] Interview with a participant at the meeting, Phnom Penh, November 1998.

[2] See, for example, Eva Mysliwiec, *Punishing the Poor: The International Isolation of Kampuchea* (Oxford: OXFAM, 1988), on the effects of international embargo on aid to Cambodia in the 1980s.

[3] Quoted by Barbara Crossette, 'The World Expected Peace. It Found a New Brutality,' *New York Times*, 24 January 1999, Section 4, pp. 1, 16.

[4] Michael Bryans, Bruce D. Jones and Janice Gross Stein, 'Mean Times: Humanitarian Action in Complex Political Emergencies – Stark Choice, Cruel Dilemmas,' Report of the NGOs in Complex Emergencies Project, Center for International Studies, University of Toronto, January 1999, p. 39.

[5] Ben Barber, 'Feeding Refugees, or War? The Dilemma of Humanitarian Aid,' *Foreign Affairs*, vol. 76, no. 4, July/August 1997, p. 9.

[6] Bob Devecchi of the International Rescue Committee, quoted by Barber, p. 11.

[7] Michael Ignatieff, 'The Stories We Tell: Television and Humanitarian Aid,' in Jonathan Moore, ed., *Hard Choices: Moral Dilemmas in Humanitarian Intervention* (Lanham, MD: Rowman & Littlefield, 1998), p. 298. See also Brauman, p. 191.

[8] Rony Brauman, 'Refugee Camps, Population Transfers, and NGOs,' in Jonathan Moore, ed., *Hard Choices: Moral Dilemmas in Humanitarian Intervention* (Lanham, MD: Rowman & Littlefield, 1998), pp. 191–2.

[9] Ian Martin, 'Hard Choices after Genocide: Human Rights and Political Failures in Rwanda,' in Jonathan Moore, ed., *Hard Choices: Moral Dilemmas in Humanitarian Intervention* (Lanham, MD: Rowman & Littlefield, 1998), p. 167.

[10] Nicholas Stockton, 'In Defence of Humanitarianism,' *Disasters*, vol. 22, no. 4, December 1998, pp. 354–6.

[11] Mary Anderson, 'You Save My Life Today, But for What Tomorrow?' in Jonathan Moore, ed., *Hard Choices: Moral Dilemmas in Humanitarian Intervention* (Lanham, MD: Rowman & Littlefield, 1998), pp. 137–56.

[12] George A. Lopez and David Cortright, 'Financial Sanctions: The Key to a "Smart" Sanctions Strategy,' *Die Friedens-Warte*, vol. 72, no. 4, 1997, p. 329.

[13] Political declaration from the Ministerial Meeting of the Steering Board of the Peace Implementation Council, Sintra, Portugal, 30 May 1997, paragraph 45. In addition to the High Representative, members of the ETF include the resident representatives of the World Bank, EU, EBRD, and USAID.

[14] Personal interviews with NGO fieldworkers in Bosnia, June 1998. Similar manipulation was reportedly common in Bosnia's Serb Republic; see Radha Kumar, *Divide and Fall? Bosnia in the Annals of Partition* (London: Verso, 1997), pp. 123–4.

15 SFOR, 'Transcript of the Press Conference held on 14 January 1997' (available on the worldwide web at: http:/www.nato.int).

16 'G-8 Will Deny Loans to India and Pakistan,' *International Herald Tribune*, 13–14 June 1998, p. 2.

Chapter 5

1 Kofi Annan, 'Help by Rewarding Good Governance,' *International Herald Tribune*, 20 March 2002, p. 8.

2 See, for example, Gerard Prunier, *The Rwanda Crisis: History of a Genocide* (New York: Columbia University Press, 1995).

3 Tony Smith, 'Recipe for Disaster?' *French Politics & Society*, vol. 14, no. 3, Summer 1996, p. 64.

4 World Bank, *Assessing Aid: What Works, What Doesn't, and Why* (Oxford: Oxford University Press, 1998), p. 40.

5 *Ibid.*, p. 1.

6 Leonce Ndikumana and James K. Boyce, 'Congo's Odious Debt: External Borrowing and Capital Flight in Zaire,' *Development and Change*, vol. 29, no. 2, 1998.

7 David Finch, 'Let the IMF be the IMF,' *International Economy*, January/February 1988, p. 127.

8 Guy de Jonquières, 'Tied aid dinosaur defies extinction,' *Financial Times*, 17 September 1996.

9 David J. Rothkopf, *The Price of Peace: Emergency Economic Intervention and U.S. Foreign Policy* (Washington DC: Carnegie Endowment, 1998), p. 78.

10 Interview with a UN human rights official, Phnom Penh, November 1998.

11 Adam Piore, 'Some in US say prime minister was behind Cambodia attack,' *The Boston Globe*, 10 October 1999, p. A35.

12 International Crisis Group, 'Minority Return or Mass Relocation?' Sarajevo, 14 May 1998, p. 10.

13 Quoted in Barton Gellman, 'Is Israel Still Under US Pressure? Maybe Yes, Maybe No, but It's Quiet Now,' *International Herald Tribune*, 20 May 1998, p. 6.

14 Steven Erlanger, 'Pro-Israel Lobby in US Wields Discreet Power,' *International Herald Tribune*, 27 August 1998, p. 2. See also Jonathan Broder, 'Netanyahu and American Jews,' *World Policy Journal*, vol. 15, no. 1, Spring 1998.

15 Personal interview with a senior international official who participated in these meetings, Gaza City, March 1998.

16 Quoted in Bob Woodward, *The Choice* (New York: Simon & Schuster, 1996), pp. 260–1. See also Mark Danner, 'The US and the Yugoslav Catastrophe,' *The New York Review of Books*, vol. 44, no. 18, 20 November 1997.

17 Michael Ignatieff, 'The Stories We Tell: Television and Humanitarian Aid,' in Jonathan Moore, ed., *Hard Choices: Moral Dilemmas in Humanitarian Intervention* (Lanham, MD: Rowman & Littlefield, 1998).

18 Nancy Sherman, 'Empathy, Respect, and Humanitarian Intervention,' *Ethics and International Affairs*, vol. 12, 1998.

19 World Bank, *Assessing Aid*, p. 10.

20 *Ibid.*, p. 142.

21 Gus Edgren, 'A Challenge to the Aid Relationship', in *Aid Dependency* (Stockholm: Swedish International Development Authority, 1996), p. 11; cited in World Bank, *Assessing Aid*, p. 117.

22 'Bosnia and Herzegovina: A New Beginning', *IMF Survey*, January 8, 1996.

23 *The World Bank's Experience with Post-conflict Reconstruction: Volume III: El Salvador Case Study* (Washington DC: World Bank,

Report No. 17769, 4 May 1998),
p. 41.

24 *The General Framework Agreement for Peace in Bosnia and Herzegovina.* Annex 10, Article II, Sections 1(a) and 1(c).

25 Personal interview, Sarajevo, September 1997.

26 James D. Wolfensohn, 'Development Aid Needs Fixing,' *International Herald Tribune*, 8 December 1999, p. 8. See also Jonathan Fox, 'The World Bank

Inspection Panel: Lessons from the First Five Years,' *Global Governance*, vol. 6, no. 3, 2000.

27 Stanley Hoffmann, *Duties Beyond Borders: On the Limits and Possibilities of Ethical International Politics* (Syracuse, New York: Syracuse University Press, 1981), pp. 26–7.

28 'Secretary-General Presents his Annual Report to General Assembly,' UN Press Release SG/SM/7136, 20 September 1999.